ENGAGEMENT ECONOMICS

Increasing
Performance & Profitability
by Engaging Your People

DIONDRA FILICETTI

Paperback ISBN: 978-1-7390782-2-5
E-book ISBN: 978-1-7390782-3-2
Hardcover ISBN: 978-1-7390782-4-9

Created By: Diondra Filicetti
Cover Design: Celine Gantioqui

Contact:
Driven By... Co.
drivenbyco.com
info@drivenbyco.com

While the author has made every effort to provide accurate internet addresses
at the time of publication, neither the publisher nor the author assumes any
responsibility for errors, or for changes that occur after publication.

Dedication

To my father, Sil Filicetti, who supported every idea and endeavour I've ever had, and whom we lost too soon.

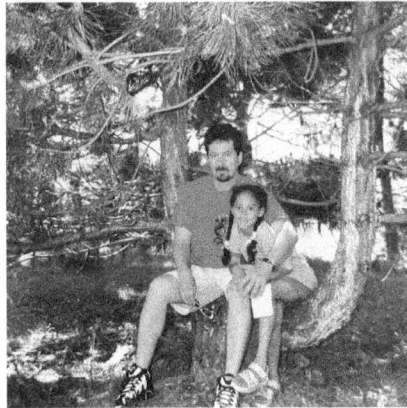

Contents

Introduction

It was a Wednesday afternoon, and I was sitting in the boardroom with my team. We were discussing a business problem: our lengthy processing times in comparison to our competitors. I had sat in this boardroom many times before, but this time I truly paid attention. When I looked around the room, I saw faces with expressions of dejection, irritation, and complete disinterest. The thing is, I was seated among people who possessed exceptional skill, a wealth of experience, and specialized expertise. Yet, we could not solve this problem. For every solution raised, a problem was presented. When it came to assigning responsibility, fingers were pointing instead of hands raising. It was evident that not a single person wanted to be there, including me. Everyone was disengaged.

It wasn't always this way. When new employees first started at that company (myself included), they were very engaged and enthusiastic about contributing to the team's mission and making a positive impact. They would take on projects that fell outside of the scope of their roles because of the big-picture benefits to the organization. However, over time, again and again, I would watch that engagement fade away. At that moment, in that Wednesday afternoon meeting, trying to improve our processing times, it finally dawned on me. We had this problem in the first place *because* we were disengaged. It was the disengagement that was impacting our performance.

I've come to realize that disengaged teams are everywhere. Disengagement is a widespread problem. What I found most interesting is that engagement is never the problem being discussed in the boardrooms. We monitor business metrics like revenue, profit, expenses, errors, and processing times. Among these metrics, employee engagement does not often make the cut. We treat employee engagement as a luxury rather than a necessity. Though, perhaps we would pay more attention if we knew the true costs of disengagement.

Gallup, a multinational analytics and advisory company, estimates that low engagement costs the global economy **USD 8.9 trillion,** or 9% of global gross domestic product (GDP).[1]

That's staggering.

That's bad economics.

In fact, that's bad *engagement* economics.

WHAT IS ENGAGEMENT ECONOMICS?

Economics is a long-standing social science that studies the production, distribution, and consumption of goods and services.[2] *Engagement* **economics** explores the relationship between employee engagement and the efficiency and effectiveness of the production / distribution of goods and services. Therefore, as a definition for this book, *engagement economics* **is the social science that studies how employee engagement ultimately impacts performance and profitability.**

Whether or not our employees are engaged plays a major role in how much effort they bring to their work. It affects how well they communicate and collaborate with others and, ultimately, how committed they are to the success of the organization. When they are disengaged, they bring less effort to work, create friction in communication and collaboration, and are less committed. There are many costs associated with that reduction in effort. Therefore, in today's fast-paced economy, it's not enough to focus on strategy and systems alone. Our greatest asset is our people.

Too many leaders overlook this simple truth: Engaged employees drive better performance and profitability results. And with such significant global economic losses in disengagement, it is clear that we're not doing enough to support engagement.

We often think about engagement in terms of individual initiatives such as hosting a team-building day, creating flex hours, or offering free coffee and snacks. While these are all nice to have, they are often implemented as one-off disconnected strategies as opposed to a more comprehensive or systemic engagement strategy, which should address your team's fundamental needs for engagement. Being offered free coffee while having to work in a disrespectful environment does not support engagement, in the same way that giving water to a person who is hungry does not address their needs.

From my realization in the boardroom that disengagement was the source of our issues, I wondered, *What do our teams need in order to be engaged*? How do we maintain the enthusiasm of the new hires so that they continue to contribute and *solve challenges* instead of *challenge solutions*? What are the conditions that would strengthen and not stifle employee engagement?

We can start by comparing the difference in engagement outcomes when you put the same person on two different teams.

Same Person, Different Team, Different Outcome

In one school of thought, one's success is driven by their own internal characteristics: determination, resilience, discipline, and creativity. These are certainly the qualities of successful people. However, to what extent does one's team determine one's performance? It brings us back to the old nature vs. nurture argument.

I once observed a business development specialist who, by nature, held the qualities for success. He was a hard worker, an effective communicator, and diligent in his efforts to bring in new clients. He was responsible for managing and growing a national portfolio of more than eighty clients. His efforts, however, were only somewhat effective. His team lacked trust in him, and they also had an unwillingness to adapt to the needs of new clients. The team's manager was unsupportive and preferred not to get involved with team dynamics. The team was disengaged and wanted to do things the way they had always been done. They created friction in the process of onboarding new clients, significantly slowing down the efforts of this business development specialist. His performance did not just reflect his own abilities; it was a reflection of the entire team's ability to work together.

Unsurprisingly, he quit.

Shortly after, he was hired by a company that was the complete opposite: high levels of engagement, a willingness to adapt, and led by a supportive manager who encouraged the team to try new ways to achieve organizational goals. All of a sudden, this business development specialist's ideas were innovative, not "annoying." They collaborated to come up with new solutions instead of trying to find reasons not to change. On this team, his efforts in business development were successful and his performance had never been better. In this case, his performance was accelerated and not hindered by his team.

On the other hand, there was someone I knew when I was in high school. We'll call him Barry. Barry, by all characteristics, was a low performer. He was undisciplined, unmotivated, prone to procrastination, avoided responsibility, and was easily distracted. Years later, I ran into Barry at a wedding, where he told me about his new job. It was as if I were talking to a completely different person. This Barry was engaged, excited, and focused. He shared that his boss genuinely believed in him, providing guidance and coaching to help him succeed in sales. It was clear to see that Barry had found the right team. He was finally getting what he needed to support his performance.

Team engagement, leadership, and performance are all inextricably linked.

If we fulfill our team's engagement needs, we will see a difference in their performance. That improved performance ultimately contributes to the profitability of the organization. This is **positive engagement economics**.

Before writing this book, I had the honour of delivering two TEDx Talks on how to develop engaged and motivated teams. While those presentations sparked meaningful conversations, I quickly realized they weren't enough. Leaders needed more than inspiration—they also needed a practical, in-depth guide they could implement in real life. Even the training sessions I led afterwards could only scratch the surface in the couple of hours we had. That's why I wrote this book—to give leaders a clear, actionable roadmap to build high-performing, deeply engaged teams, and to get out of those miserable Wednesday afternoon meetings. This book explores our teams' engagement needs and provides you, as a leader, a priority framework to assess where your team is at and what might be missing. It also includes strategies for implementation, best practices, and examples of success.

People, and most especially groups of people, are highly nuanced, which makes leadership a challenge. However, as leaders, we have the power to engage our people and build high-performing teams. First, we need an understanding of **engagement economics**.

Chapter 1: Defining Engagement Economics

Henry Ford, an American inventor, businessman, and founder of Ford Motor Co., made industrial innovations that had a profound economic impact. Among his innovations was the moving assembly line method of production, which significantly sped up production.[3] Before that, manufacturing was largely done by manual assembly. Workers moved around the car as it sat stationary, assembling parts one by one. Production was slow and costly, making cars a luxury item only affordable to the wealthy elite. Ford's introduction of the assembly line in 1913 transformed this model entirely. By having cars move along a conveyor belt, with each worker assigned to a specific, repetitive task, Ford reduced the production time of the famous Model T vehicle from twelve hours per car to just ninety minutes. This not only slashed manufacturing costs but also made cars—particularly the Model T—affordable and accessible to the general public. The assembly line reshaped the automobile industry and consumer culture at large.

The problem was that workers hated it. Their work became boring and repetitive. Many workers left to find jobs with competitors. The high turnover problem was becoming a productivity issue as it interrupted operations. Without knowing it at the time, Henry Ford turned to employee satisfaction initiatives to persuade workers to stay with the company. He reduced the number of working hours to popularize the forty-hour work week, increasing work-life balance and quality of life for Ford employees. He also implemented the five-dollar workday compensation structure, which was more than double the worker's regular daily wage at the time.[4] As a result, mechanics from around the country headed to Detroit (where Ford was headquartered) in pursuit of these high wages. These employee satisfaction initiatives made factory operations substantially more efficient, gave the company a significant hiring advantage, and increased employee retention.[5]

Rarely in business does a problem become a priority until it has a financial consequence—whether positive or negative. Decisions are driven by the potential for financial gain or the risk of financial loss, whether in the short or long term. When there's no link to financial viability, these items fall lower or even right off the priority list.

Although employee satisfaction initiatives were used by business owners like Henry Ford to improve performance, the term "employee satisfaction" did not become a topic of interest until after the Hawthorne study, which took place at a General Electric factory from 1924 to 1932.

EMPLOYEE SATISFACTION VS. EMPLOYEE EXPERIENCE VS. EMPLOYEE ENGAGEMENT

General Electric (GE) was a major manufacturer of lightbulbs. In an effort to increase lightbulb sales, GE wanted to scientifically prove that better workplace lighting would improve worker productivity. To do so, they provided $50,000 to the Committee on Industrial Lighting (CIL), a division of the National Research Council. The Western Electric Hawthorne Plant in Cicero, Illinois, was chosen as the testing site.[6] The hypothesis was that increased illumination of the workspace would result in an increase in productivity. The study, however, failed to show any relationship between improved lighting and productivity. What they did discover however, was that being observed and getting increased attention from supervisors improved job performance.[7] These findings led to further experiments on the impact of other employee satisfaction measures on performance. These studies revealed the importance of social and psychological factors in employee morale—later reframed as "employee satisfaction."

Employee satisfaction is defined as the level of contentment employees feel towards their job. It is concerned with whether an employee is satisfied with the work they do, the pay and benefits they receive, and their work environment. Therefore, in other words, employee satisfaction is a measure of how well the employer has met the minimum needs of the employees in order to keep them content.

A focus on **employee experience** is replacing employee satisfaction. No longer are we aiming for mere satisfaction from employees; employers are taking a more holistic approach to understanding their employees' experiences at work. Employers are beginning to understand that a satisfied employee is not necessarily an engaged employee.

Instead of asking whether an employee is satisfied with the basics of their job, employee experience is concerned with the quality of the interactions between the employee and employer. It looks at things like onboarding efficiency, employee growth over time, the quality of relationships the employee has with colleagues, and their overall sentiments about their work. Employee experience looks at the relationship between the employee and employer and is a key component in contributing to employee engagement.

The distinction between employee satisfaction and employee experience is essential. While employee satisfaction is largely one-sided—focusing on whether the organization meets the individual's needs—employee experience focuses on relationships, emphasizing how both the employee and employer shape the workplace together.

Employee engagement goes a step further, reflecting the depth of an employee's commitment to actively contributing towards shared goals and the organization's success.

In short,

- **Employee Satisfaction = What are you (the employer) doing for me?**
- **Employee Experience = How are we doing things together?**
- **Employee Engagement = How committed am I (the employee) to contributing to our shared goals?**

When looking to increase performance, we'll explore why employee experience and employee engagement are far more effective than only monitoring employee satisfaction.

WHAT DOES ENGAGEMENT REALLY MEAN?

When I was hired for my first full-time job after my university graduation, my excitement was at an all-time high. This excitement to join the working world for the first time is something you can likely recall from your first job. I remember not knowing what to expect, but I knew that I would do every-thing in my power to make an impact. I bought all new work attire, new shoes, and a new bag to carry all the important documents I needed. When meeting my colleagues for the first time, I shook their hands with a huge smile on my face, eager to show that I was committed to being a strong and sup-portive collaborator on the team. I sat wide-eyed in the training sessions, fas-cinated by the work and structures in place. Although I didn't have to, I would take reading materials home and spend my own time getting familiar with procedures so I could be more productive at work and be more present in the training. The training process was one of the best I had experienced: a combination of in-class training, e-learning, reading, and on-the-job training. The on-the-job training involved spending one to two weeks in every depart-ment to get a real grasp of what everyone was responsible for. At the end of the training period, you worked with your direct manager to build a three-year growth plan for your progression in the company. Because this company was international, there was even the possibility of transferring to different sites. The positive experience and excitement about future potential filled me with enthusiasm and inspired me to bring my best effort to work every day. The point being, **I was highly engaged.** I was ready and willing to give it my all each and every day, bringing 110% effort.

Discretionary Effort Model

Some team members are willing to do only the bare minimum. They focus strictly on the tasks that fall within the list of their job responsibilities. These are the "that's not in my job description" folks. This reluctance to go beyond their defined roles creates tension with the team members who are committed to doing all they can for the sake of the team's success. The cause of this tension is a mismatch in what's called **discretionary effort**.

Discretionary effort is the level of effort team members are willing to give that goes beyond the minimum responsibilities of their role. It asks the question: How much more than the bare minimum are your team members willing to do? We can map it as the difference between what team members have to do vs. what they want to do.

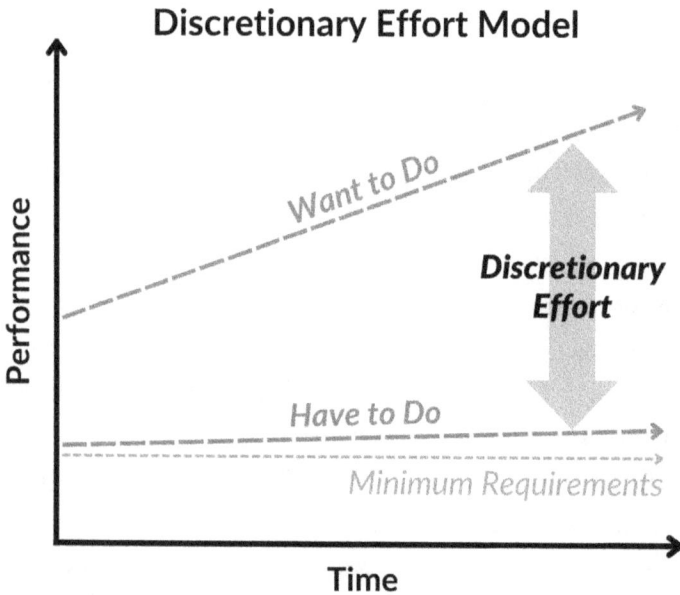

Discretionary Effort Model

Performance

Want to Do

Discretionary
Effort

Have to Do

Minimum Requirements

Time

High performance comes from shifting your team from merely showing up to maximizing discretionary effort. It's about moving output from "good enough" to "great."[8] **When discretionary effort is maximized, organizations experience positive *engagement economics*.**

As one would expect, the additional discretionary effort is directly related to an increase in performance. In fact, a 2020 Gallup global study revealed that business units with engaged employees, who often exert more discretionary effort, experience a 10% improvement in customer metrics and a 23% increase in profitability compared to units with lower engagement levels.[9] Gallup found that employees who exert additional discretionary effort have higher productivity rates (18%) as they handle tasks more efficiently and effectively.[10]

When thinking of a practical definition and measurement of employee engagement, discretionary effort is a good measure.

In short,

Engagement = MORE discretionary effort	Disengagement = LESS discretionary effort
More effort means: • More communication • More collaboration • More commitment	Less effort means: • Less communication • Less collaboration • Less commitment

In an engagement study conducted by Psychometrics in 2011, 368 Canadian human resources (HR) professionals working in business, government, consulting, education, and not-for-profit organizations were surveyed about workplace engagement.[11] To the 368 HR professionals, the research team posed the question: What is the most common result of engaged employees?

These HR professionals reported that the most common results of engaged employees were a willingness to do more than expected (discretionary effort), higher productivity, better working relationships, more satisfied customers, and greater loyalty to the organization.

What is the most common result of engaged employees?

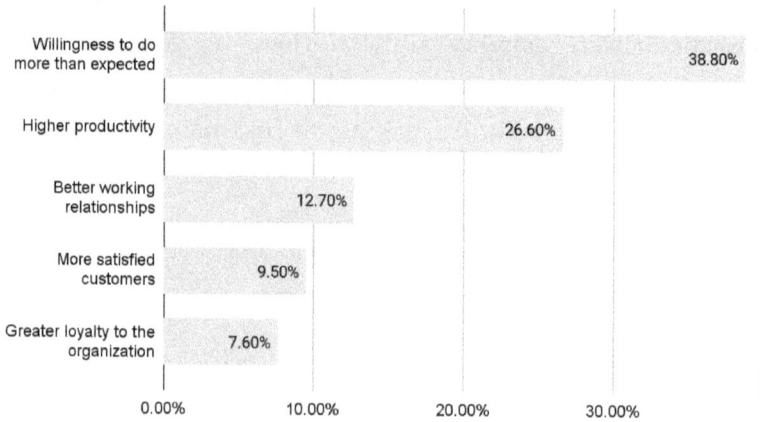

Category	Percentage
Willingness to do more than expected	38.80%
Higher productivity	26.60%
Better working relationships	12.70%
More satisfied customers	9.50%
Greater loyalty to the organization	7.60%

These outcomes significantly enhance both individual and team performance, creating a positive cycle of success. As a result, employee engagement is a key driver of organizational growth. This highlights its essential role in fostering a high-performing team.

In the same study, the research team posed the question, What is the most common result of **disengaged** employees?

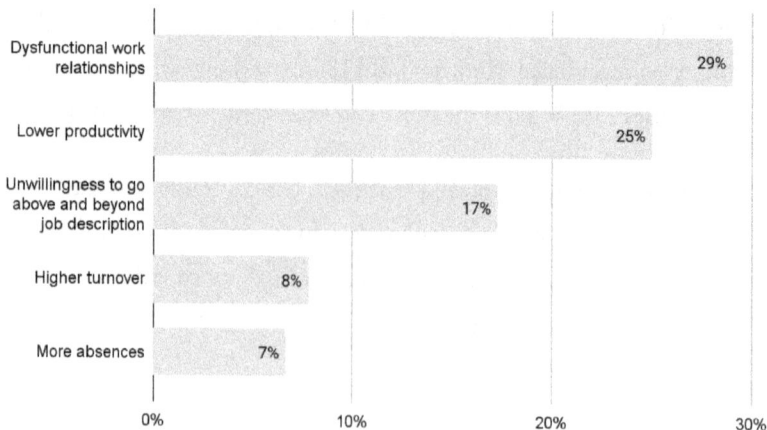

What is the most common result of disengaged employees?

Category	Percentage
Dysfunctional work relationships	29%
Lower productivity	25%
Unwillingness to go above and beyond job description	17%
Higher turnover	8%
More absences	7%

One might expect that the most common result of disengaged employees would be the direct opposite of engaged employees—an unwillingness to do more than expected. The result of disengaged employees however, is far worse. Before an unwillingness to go above and beyond the job description, disengaged employees create dysfunctional work relationships and lower productivity. If disengaged teams create a decrease in productivity and damage working relationships, there will be a damaging impact on the organization far beyond the immediate effects. It results in **negative engagement economics**.

The outcome of "dysfunctional work relationships" from the Psychometrics study is worrisome. If you've ever been around people in a dysfunctional relationship, you'll know first-hand that dysfunctional relationships affect everyone. Somehow even the people outside of the relationship are sucked into the drama. The same occurs at work.

I was once tasked with trying to identify why one department in an organization had such different levels of engagement than the rest. The estimating department had a bad reputation for being difficult to work with and constantly slowing down projects. So, I spent some time there to observe what was happening on a daily basis. One employee—we'll call him Darren—had worked as part of the estimating team for over ten years. He was highly skilled but known to be irritable. At the time, a new member—Julia—had just joined the team, so I was able to witness the onboarding process. Although Darren was not directly responsible for onboarding or training Julia, Julia needed to consult Darren daily for support. Their roles were interconnected. While answering Julia's questions, Darren expressed his frustrations about the other departments. He constantly told her how other departments continuously overlooked information, didn't follow procedure, and expected him to deliver estimates without first providing all the information, just to get projects to move faster. Darren often used phrases like "That's not in my job description," or "That's not what it says in the procedure, so that's not how it's going to go."

Having set this expectation in Julia's mind, she started to share the same sentiments about the other departments. Her interactions with the other departments began to take a tone of frustration. Eventually, just like the rest of the estimating team, Julia sought to point out all the problems in projects and adopted the belief that the rest of the organization was incompetent. This general belief held by everyone on the estimating team inadvertently caused them to avoid collaboration and present problems for potential solutions, slowing down productivity. (Estimates were turned around in days instead of hours.)

From the perspective of the other departments, many of the details about projects were not always available at the time the organization was asked by the customer to present a solution. The sales and customer service teams wanted to move forward on coming up with solutions with the information that they *did* have in order to be more agile and innovative for their customers.

It was a matter of weeks for a new hire to share the belief system and demeanour of one of the most actively disengaged members of the organization. **Everyone can justify their disengagement**, and for that reason, disengagement spreads. This process can be long or short, noticeable or unnoticeable, as the daily interactions between employees accrue to their overall experience. When those interactions are constantly negative, the disengagement disease starts to spread and infect other areas of the organization.

Engagement Categories

Gallup's research on engagement revealed that employees typically fall into one of three categories: engaged, not engaged, or actively disengaged. Each has unique characteristics in the workplace.

Engaged
- They are highly involved and enthusiastic.
- They are drivers of performance and innovation.

Not Engaged
- They are psychologically unattached to their work and company.
- They put time but not energy or passion into their work.
- They "quietly quit."

Actively Disengaged
- They are not just unhappy, they are resentful.
- They act out their unhappiness.
- They often undermine the efforts of engaged employees.
- They "loudly quit."

In their *State of the Global Workforce Report* in 2024, Gallup surveyed employees in over 160 countries around the world to look at the current state of employee mental health and engagement at a global level. Based on their findings, they were able to map how many people fell into each of the engagement categories. When we see the numbers, it is clear we have an engagement problem.

Actively Disengaged
15%

Engaged
23%

Not Engaged
62%

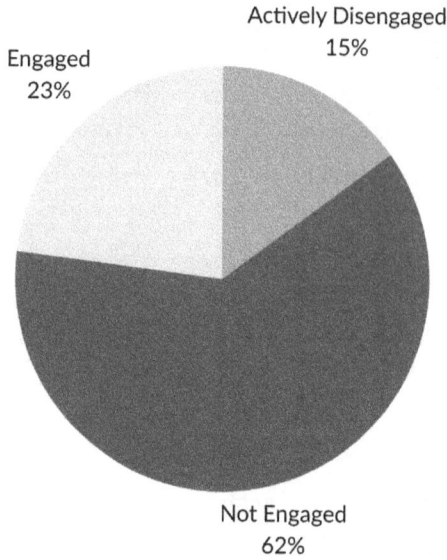

Over two-thirds of the population are not engaged, and it's costing organizations all around the world massive lost opportunity costs.

COSTS OF DISENGAGEMENT

In the US, it is estimated that the annual costs of disengagement exceed $500 billion.[12] These costs are a combination of the many behaviours of disengaged employees that contribute to reduced business performance. Some of these behaviours have costs directly associated with them and are easy to quantify, while others have an indirect and not-so-obvious cost to the organization.

Direct Costs of Disengagement	Indirect Costs of Disengagement
• **Higher Turnover Costs**: Disengaged employees are more likely to leave, leading to increased costs for recruiting, hiring, and training new employees. • **Increased Absenteeism**: Disengaged employees take more sick days, leading to productivity losses and increased reliance on temporary workers or overtime pay. • **Lower Productivity**: Employees who are not engaged contribute less effort, leading to decreased output and inefficiencies in workflow. • **Workplace Theft and Errors**: Disengaged employees may be more likely to steal from their employers or make costly mistakes due to lack of attention or motivation. • **Customer Loss**: Poor service from disengaged employees can drive customers away, reducing revenue.[13]	• **Decreased Innovation**: A disengaged workforce is less likely to contribute new ideas or engage in problem-solving, limiting the company's ability to innovate and stay competitive. • **Lower Employee Morale**: Disengaged employees negatively influence engaged employees, leading to a dysfunctional work environment and reduced teamwork. • **Poor Employer Brand and Reputation**: High disengagement levels can result in negative reviews on employer review sites, making it harder to attract top talent. • **Higher Health and Wellness Costs**: Disengaged employees experience higher stress levels, which can lead to burnout, increased health care costs, and long-term disability claims. • **Decreased Customer Loyalty**: Customers who experience poor service from disengaged employees may not only leave but also spread negative word-of-mouth, further damaging the company's reputation.

The question is then, what is disengagement costing **you**? We know the friction that disengagement causes between employees, but how does this friction directly impact the costs to the organization?

- Is it lowering productivity?
- Is it lowering customer satisfaction?
- Is it decreasing results?
- Is it increasing sick days?
- Is it increasing health / benefit spending?
- Is it wasting time?
- Is it increasing the turnover of your best team members?

The cost of disengagement is high. How high, exactly? Well, that depends on your unique situation. However, if no interventions are put in place, the disengagement disease spreads, and the costs increase exponentially.

Most employees don't start a job being disengaged. They generally lose engagement over time. The reality is that, at some point, both "not engaged" and "actively disengaged" team members have had their engagement needs overlooked or unmet. Later in this book, we will explore the needs of an engaged team and some of the things that lead team members to become not engaged or actively disengaged.

ENGAGEMENT IS GOOD FOR BUSINESS

Gallup determined that "engaged employees produce better business outcomes than other employees do—across industries, company sizes, and nationalities, and in good economic times and bad."[14] Their 2024 meta-analysis (a fancy word for a study of studies) examined over 183,000 business units across fifty-three industries in ninety countries. The findings revealed that reducing disengaged workers leads to better outcomes. Highly engaged teams achieved higher productivity, profitability, sales, and employee well-being compared to less engaged teams.[15]

It's easy to conclude that disengaged employees are less productive. Intuitively, we know that engaged employees do more, but to what degree?

Outcomes of Highly Engaged Teams

When comparing the top quartile (most engaged teams) with the bottom quartile (least engaged teams), the performance gaps were vast.[16] Within a typical organization, compared to bottom quartile teams, top quartile teams report fewer negative outcomes and more positive outcomes.

Fewer Negative Outcomes

- 78% lower absenteeism
- 21% lower turnover (for high-turnover organizations)
- 51% lower turnover (for low-turnover organizations)
- 28% less shrinkage (theft)
- 63% fewer safety incidents (accidents)
- 32% fewer quality defects

More Positive Outcomes

- 10% higher customer loyalty / engagement
- 18% higher productivity (sales)
- 14% higher productivity (production)

Greater Organizational Success

- 23% higher profitability
- 70% greater well-being
- 22% more organizational participation[17]

Increasing the engagement metric improves a variety of other key business metrics that are directly or indirectly linked to the bottom line. If it's not clear by now, engagement has a real economic impact and is not just a feel-good initiative.

Engagement is good for business.

From a management perspective, the question is, *How do I increase engagement to ultimately increase my team's performance?* But one must first ask themselves, *As a manager, am I standing in my team's way?*

Chapter 2:
Is Your Team Saying
"I Hate My Boss"?

Here's something they'll probably never teach you in business school: The single biggest decision you make in your job—bigger than all of the rest—is who you name manager. When you name the wrong person manager, nothing fixes that bad decision. Not compensation, not benefits—nothing.
—Jim Clifton, Gallup CEO 1998-2022

Many manufacturing organizations operate in multiple shifts: day shift and night shift. Generally, each shift has its own group of equipment operators, quality control representatives, and supervisors. After observing the engagement dynamics at one manufacturing organization in particular, I noticed that the day shift workers were excessively stressed out and dejected. The night shift workers, although also high-strung, were much more positive and enthusiastic. How could two teams operating under the same workplace standards and procedures have such different levels of engagement? The answer became clear when someone from day shift requested a transfer to night shift. This came as a surprise because most people want to transfer *from* night shift *to* day shift in order to have a more normal sleep schedule and better work-life balance. Someone requesting the opposite was strange. It turned out that they wanted to get away from their direct supervisor and were willing to change their whole lifestyle to do so.

You've likely heard the saying that "people leave managers, not companies." Even if a company is a great place to work, a manager may be impossible to work for. According to a Gallup study, at some point in their career, **one in two** employees have left a job to get away from a manager and improve their overall life.[18] The impact of bad managers spans further than just turnover.

Before we begin to invest in any engagement initiatives, we must first determine whether the manager will be a help or a hindrance to those efforts.

BAD BOSSES, BAD FOR THE BOTTOM LINE

Most people spend more time at work than they do with their families. Think about it. When you factor in commuting time, errands, and regular responsibilities, there's not a whole lot of time left outside of work. So, it's no surprise that more than half of worldwide employees say that their job is the biggest factor influencing their mental health. Just by nature of frequency and proximity, managers have a greater impact on our mental health than doctors and therapists. Their influence is even equal to that of our spouses and partners.[19] With that much influence, managers have a great responsibility.

Companies spend hundreds of millions of dollars on health benefits, yet the actions of a poor manager can negate the positive effects of the company's benefit programs.

So, before we talk about engagement needs, it's important to rethink your management strategy.

MANAGER'S IMPACT ON ENGAGEMENT

For every story I've heard about a great leader, I've heard fifty stories about a horrible boss. Even if we haven't experienced a horrible boss ourselves, we certainly know someone who has. They're seemingly everywhere. Even in the movies. If you have ever seen *Horrible Bosses* or *The Devil Wears Prada*, you have witnessed just how much a boss can disrupt an employee's life. Bosses have the ability to make your life hell. Their behaviour, communication style, and management decisions have a direct influence on your work environment, career trajectory, and engagement.

Before considering other factors, it is essential to recognize that one of the most significant drivers of employee engagement is an employee's relationship with their direct manager. In fact, according to Gallup's *State of the American Manager Report*, **managers account for at least 70% of the variance in employee engagement scores. Failing to develop leaders is a costly mistake.**[20]

What Are Managers Doing that Reduces Engagement?

An HR organization conducted a study where they asked more than 1,000 US-based employees to rate various bad boss behaviours. With this data, they generated the "Bad Boss Index." According to this index and other reports of bad boss behaviour, the most problematic behaviours from managers are:

- Management Style / Micromanaging
- Lack of Recognition / Taking Credit for Employee Work
- Condescending Attitude / Lack of Empathy

These behaviours are among the top characteristics of bosses that create dis-engagement and are ultimately the reasons people leave their jobs.[21] As you and I both know, this list doesn't begin to cover the plethora of bad behaviour an employee might experience from their manager. If I tasked you with creating a list of bad manager behaviour, I'm certain you could come up with at least ten items in under five minutes. We're all too familiar with bad boss behaviour, which in many ways is concerning. I don't think their behaviour is intentional, but it certainly illuminates underlying problems with leadership.

With great power comes great responsibility. —Uncle Ben

Maybe They're Not Bad, Just Unprepared

I don't think anybody aspires to be a horrible boss. Nobody walks into work each day thinking, How can I create more disengagement on my team? After being promoted to a management position, people generally wonder, *How can I get my team to achieve the results that my upper management is looking for?* Somewhere in the attempt to produce those results, managers—often without even realizing it—exhibit behaviours that damage employee engagement. Employees believe that managers should know better, but the reality is that many managers are woefully unprepared. In a nationwide study of over 2,000 US employers, more than half reported that they did not receive any management training, and more than one-quarter (26%) of managers said they weren't ready to become leaders when they started managing others.[22] As a matter of fact, only about one in ten people possess the high talent needed to effectively manage a team.[23] Most managers have never learned leadership skills.

In truth, this makes sense. For a moment, think about how most managers come to be in leadership positions. Leaders are not being hired out of the graduating class at "Leadership School." Managers are often promoted not for their leadership skills but instead based on the following:

- **Performance**: As a team member, they were an individual high performer.
- **Tenure**: They have been a part of the team for a long time.
- **Relationships**: They have a great relationship with upper management.

The focus on performance, tenure, and relationships does not necessarily correlate with how well the leader can develop, engage, and lead their team. Leadership comes with its own set of unique challenges.

UNIVERSAL LEADERSHIP CHALLENGES

I would consider myself an over-packer. Generally, when I pack my suitcase for a trip, it's messy and packed full of "just in case" outfits. That changed when I saw somebody open their suitcase containing their items neatly separated into small packing cubes. Recognizing that this might solve all my problems, I went online that very night to shop for packing cubes in my favourite colour. Within thirty minutes, I had ordered a set of compression packing cubes in a bright turquoise colour. The very next day it showed up on my doorstep.

The global economy is more connected than ever. For the consumer, it is as simple as searching for what you want online, entering a few details, and placing an order. But behind this transaction is a massive logistical network that connects suppliers and vendors from all over the world. To get me my packing cubes the day after I ordered them, several organizations performed several steps correctly.

Today, consumers have access to products all over the world and an expectation that they can be ordered and delivered quickly. Meeting this expectation means that several organizations must deliver high performance. Leaders from around the world are responsible for that. In such a global, interconnected economy, one might wonder just how different it might be to lead a team in America vs. Japan, for instance. How different—or similar—are the challenges faced by leaders?

The Center for Creative Leadership (CCL) conducted a study where they interviewed 763 people in leadership positions in economies all over the world. The CCL recognized that leadership is not easy and requires navigating a complex economic landscape while developing teams to deliver on objectives. Through their findings, they sought to help practicing leaders understand what they and others around the world were going through, but they also wanted to inform training and development initiatives.

The research examined leaders from China / Hong Kong, Egypt, India, Singapore, Spain, the United Kingdom, and the United States. These countries are vastly different in culture, political systems, economic structures, historical influences, social norms, and leadership styles. Despite all these differences, the challenges faced by leaders are shockingly similar.

Out of those 763 participants, there were six main challenges that appeared the most frequently. Organizations, especially those that operate internationally, contend with a complex global environment where they must manage the requirements of the government, keep up with competitors, achieve growth, and meet the expectations of stakeholders.[24] Yet, leadership challenges of this nature didn't make the list.

The top six most common challenges in order of frequency were:

- Developing managerial effectiveness
- Inspiring others
- Developing employees
- Leading a team
- Guiding change
- Managing internal stakeholders and politics

Based on this list, it would seem that the operational and business responsibilities of leaders are what they are most prepared for. The interpersonal challenges of leadership are where they are least prepared.

What's most interesting is that three out of those six challenges are directly related to engagement:

- Inspiring others
- Developing employees
- Leading a team

Inspiring others is the challenge of motivating or encouraging others to perform at higher levels and also to ensure they are satisfied with their jobs. *Developing employees* is the challenge of enhancing the skills, knowledge, abilities, and performance of individuals within the organization. This requires leadership involvement in some form of mentorship, coaching, or training. *Leading a team* is the challenge of team building and team management that ensures that individuals collaborate effectively to achieve a common goal. All three of these challenges seek the outcome of engaged and high-performing teams.

Universal Challenges Stem from Team Uniqueness

As a leader, you are faced with managing a group of people with different personalities, perspectives, interests, approaches, values, and backgrounds. Learning the unique characteristics of each team member and how they fit into the fabric of your team's objectives requires leaders to take a strategic approach to building their team.

For a moment, I want to expand our lens and look at just how universal these leadership challenges are. Perhaps we can draw a comparison between leadership in some aspects of our lives and leading employees.

When we use the term "leader," we generally picture political figures or management / executives at large corporate organizations. However, leadership roles exist in our lives outside of work. There are leaders all around us, and chances are that you're reading this book because you're one of them. A leader is anyone who is responsible for or directs others. The most common and overlooked example of an everyday leader is a parent.

Parents, like leaders, set expectations for their children's behaviour, instill values that drive decision-making, and guide their children into becoming the best (or most high-performing) version of themselves possible. Parents are highly aware of the unique characteristics that make their children different and will often have to adjust their approach based on the characteristics of the child. This adaptation is intuitive and instinctual as a parent but not so much as a leader in business. Parents know that children may not be able to communicate effectively, so parenting also requires social-emotional awareness. This awareness helps parents determine how their children are feeling in order to determine how those children need to be supported. That being said, parents often play the role of cheerleader and mentor for the kids, *inspiring them*. Parents teach and coach their kids, **developing them** and their skills. Parents are also charged with managing the entire family unit, determining how best to work together to succeed as a family, or in other words, *leading the family*.

When in the role of a parent, these universal leadership challenges seem to come more naturally than when in the role of a business leader, though they are equally important. Perhaps it's because we feel a greater sense of accountability towards our children, or perhaps we assume that because we pay employees, they are obligated to perform to the best of their ability. Fundamentally, however, both types of teams, no matter how unique they are, have universal needs, which is the very reason why there are universal leadership challenges.

Although the Center for Creative Leadership conducted research only in the realm of business leadership, the general sentiment was that any training these leaders had did not prepare them for the challenges they faced in their roles. With a direct impact on employee engagement and, ultimately, performance and profitability, leadership development is not a nice-to-have; it's a must. It is a critical business strategy. But where do we begin? For starters, if leaders had a better understanding of the universal needs of teams, they would be better positioned to tackle these universal leadership challenges.

The most valuable player is the one who makes the most players valuable. —Peyton Manning

Chapter 3:
What Does Your Team
Need?

I completed my undergraduate degree at what was then known as Ryerson University in Toronto. Like most post-secondary programs, we were given the option to select elective courses to explore different subjects and interests outside of our degree. I found myself drawn to psychology. I wanted to better understand human motivation and what drove human behaviour, especially when that behaviour seemed illogical. In my first year, I decided to take Introduction to Psychology as my elective course. I recall sitting in the lecture hall, learning about a variety of psychological theories throughout history. All these theories seemed valid in certain contexts, but none seemed to have the ability to be universally applied. That was until the professor introduced us to a framework that categorized the universal human needs that drive our decisions. The light bulb went off. Our **needs** drive our behaviour. And at the end of the day, we all have the same fundamental needs. Suddenly, I was able to attribute all types of behaviour I had witnessed in the past to an unsatisfied need within this framework. It was simple and intuitive. So rather than examining a complex psychosocial situation from an experimental lens, first, we could simply ask, *Have their needs been satisfied?*

If you've ever taken a psychology or sociology course, you are likely familiar with Maslow's Hierarchy of Needs. If not, let me bring you up to speed. Maslow's Hierarchy of Needs refers to a theory of motivation that states that five universal levels of human needs dictate human behaviour.[25] The hierarchy looks like this:

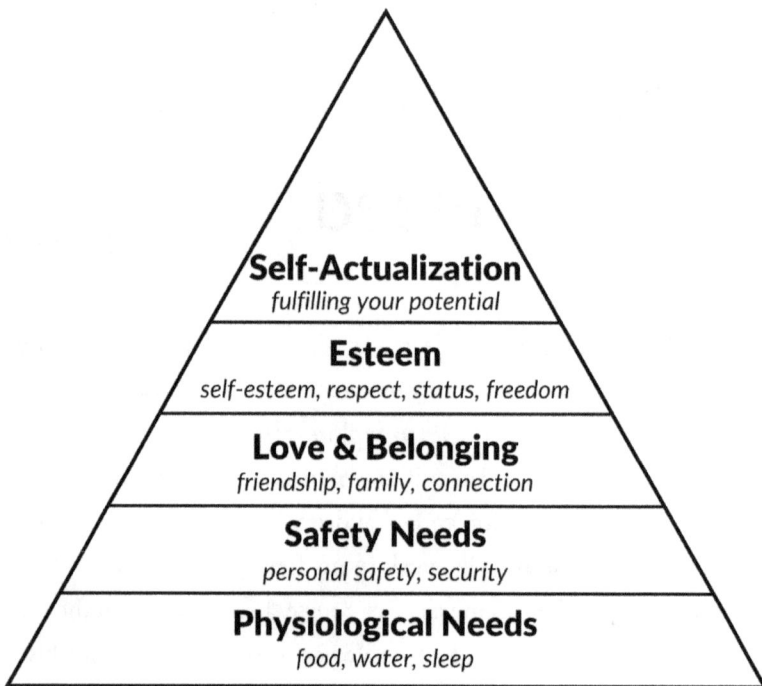

Self-Actualization
fulfilling your potential

Esteem
self-esteem, respect, status, freedom

Love & Belonging
friendship, family, connection

Safety Needs
personal safety, security

Physiological Needs
food, water, sleep

Maslow's theory suggests that lower-ranking needs in the hierarchy must be satisfied before humans can attend to needs higher up in the hierarchy. For example, if our safety needs—personal safety and security—are not satisfied, we will not have the capacity to be concerned with self-actualization. All the needs in this hierarchy contribute to our overall fulfillment and satisfaction in life, however we pursue them in order of **priority**. That priority is determined by the impact of the need being **unmet**. For example, if our need for food and water is unmet, there is a high detrimental impact on our health and well-being. Therefore, physiological needs are the first priority. According to this framework, the highest-level need that we can pursue is self-actualization. Self-actualization involves the pursuit of personal goals, the realization of one's unique talents, and the development of a sense of fulfillment and meaning in life. Many individuals never reach self-actualization because they are busy satisfying their other needs.

Maslow's Hierarchy of Needs has been incredibly useful in analyzing human behaviour throughout history and even today, as the evolution of societies reflects the increasing complexity of human needs in the hierarchy. However, the needs within Maslow's Hierarchy are individualistic. They relate to the needs of the individual as opposed to the needs of a group or team.

When looking at what universal needs must be met in order to build an engaged and high-performing team and address many of the universal leadership challenges, it requires a slightly less individualistic approach. When we're organized into teams, our needs as a collective unit are different from our needs as individuals. Our needs shift from being about our personal satisfaction and fulfillment to the conditions that allow us to work well together. **An understanding of the universal needs of a team can assist leaders in ensuring their team's needs are met.**

After analyzing engagement economics and the characteristics of engaged teams, I discovered many team needs. There are also several existing frameworks and approaches that narrow in on a few team needs, but again, these frameworks seemingly lack universality. They also failed to establish priority based on the relative impact of the unmet needs. So, after careful analysis of team dynamics, high-performance teams, and the impact of leadership, I found that team needs can be categorized into three levels. Similar to

Maslow's Hierarchy of Needs, in that each level of the hierarchy must be satisfied before addressing higher levels, I present to you a hierarchy of needs for engaged teams. It outlines the fundamental to the more complex needs that contribute to team engagement. Let's call it, ***Filicetti's Hierarchy of Team Engagement Needs*** (apologies for wordiness). However, this hierarchy intends to provide leaders with a framework to build more engaged teams, especially when leadership training is lacking.

I'll first briefly introduce the three main levels, and then, over the following chapters, I'll break each level down to identify specific team needs and what to look for. I've included real-world examples from Fortune 500 companies, smaller organizations, and my first-hand experience.

INTRODUCING FILICETTI'S HIERARCHY OF TEAM ENGAGEMENT NEEDS

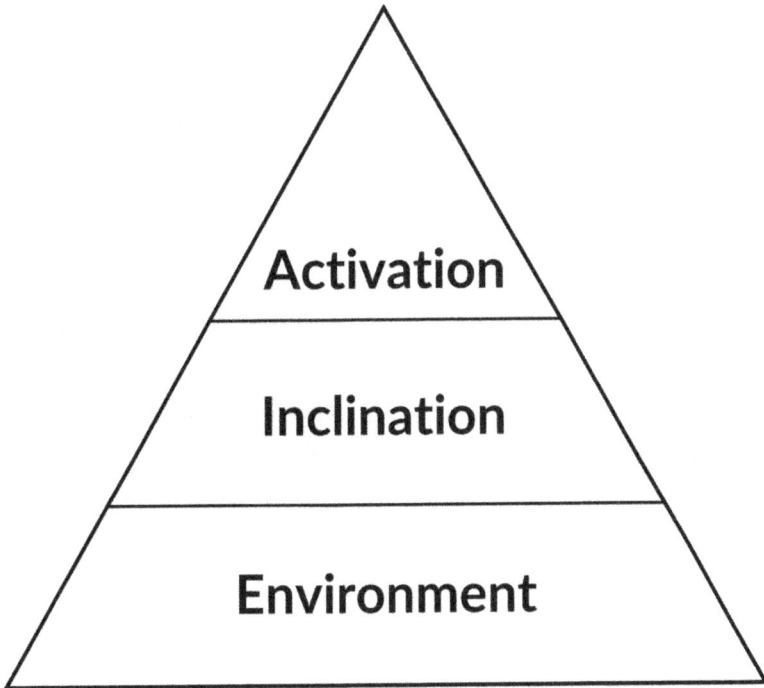

This Hierarchy of Team Engagement Needs contains three layers:

- **Environment**: the conditions of the psychosocial environment in which the team operates
- **Inclination**: how well aligned a person's abilities, interests, and values are with the role
- **Activation**: turning potential into initiative by creating a desire to take action

For the deepest levels of engagement, these three needs should be satisfied in this order. Building engagement and high performance begins with creating the right **environment,** then satisfying **inclination** by aligning the team to their roles and, finally, **activating** them to take the initiative towards their potential. Focusing on activation and inclination in an environment that promotes *dis*engagement is futile. Inclination and activation cannot overcome the need for the right conditions that set the team up for success. Even focusing on the first layer, creating an engaging environment, produces positive engagement economics. However, if you build inclination over top of a strong environment foundation, the engagement and performance results increase. As you ascend through the hierarchy, satisfying your team's needs in priority order, you will see that engagement and performance increase exponentially.

Following this framework leads to more positive engagement economics. The goal is to provide a practical approach to enhancing employee experience, enabling you to invest in the initiatives that drive lasting employee engagement. We will explore in depth the considerations that contribute to satisfying each of these team engagement needs and discuss strategies for implementation.

Where do we begin? It all begins with creating the conditions that support engagement, or in other words, the team environment.

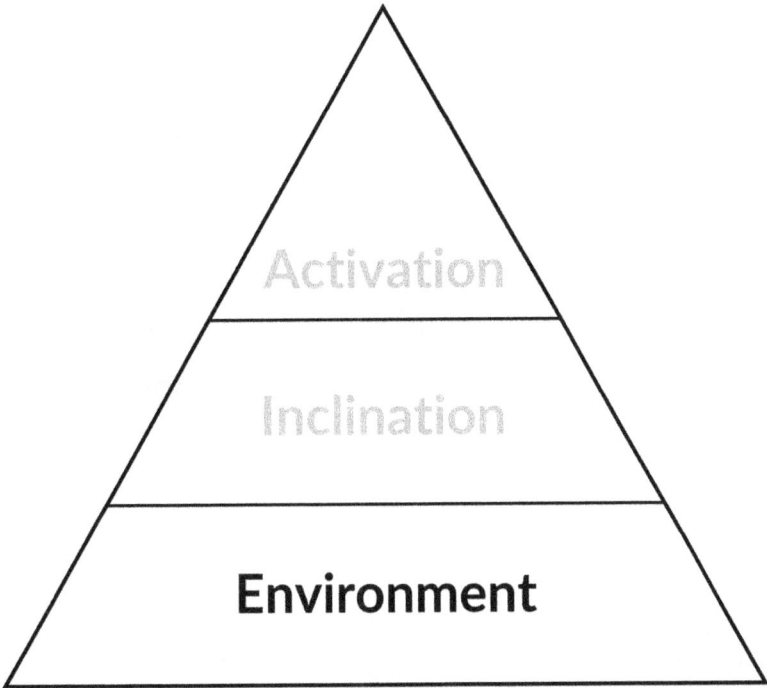

Chapter 4: Environment

Between April and September 2021, over 24 million American employees resigned from their jobs, marking the beginning of a workforce shift unlike any seen before. In 2022, a record 50.5 million people quit, according to the federal Job Openings and Labour Turnover Survey (JOLTS) report.[26] This mass wave of resignations became known as "The Great Resignation."

In 2022, the Massachusetts Institute of Technology Sloan School of Management published research giving us insight into the driving factors behind so many people's decisions to quit. One might think that low wages were to blame; however, compensation ranked only 16th among all topics that predict employee turnover.[27] The top predictor of employee turnover during The Great Resignation was a toxic corporate culture.

The most fundamental contributing factor to an engaged team is the environment in which the team operates. I intend to focus on the psychosocial characteristics in the team environment, with the assumption that the team's physical environment is safe and secure. This need sits at the base of the Hierarchy of Team Engagement Needs because **without an environment that is conducive to engagement, the other layers don't matter.**

The truth is we are, in many ways, a product of our environment. As humans, we have a natural and evolutionary tendency to adapt to our environment rather than resisting or opposing it. The term "plasticity" refers to the changes in the brain that enable an organism to adapt its behaviour in the face of changing environmental demands. The purpose of plasticity is to help the brain stay flexible so it can learn from experiences, predict what might happen next, and change actions when those predictions turn out to be wrong.[28] This ability allows us to adjust and adapt to new situations. This comes from our individual needs for safety and belonging. Early humans would have used plasticity to adapt to changing environments, learn survival skills, recognize patterns in nature, and refine hunting / gathering techniques.

Today, while adapting to our environment can still be crucial for physical safety, it has become more about maintaining social safety. For example, from our teenage years, we're familiar with the pressure to fit in. Teens might find themselves making overt changes to their clothes, their hairstyles, their activities, and even the way they speak to avoid being singled out or ridiculed for being different.

In adulthood and in the workplace, adaptations to our environment often occur subtly and subconsciously. The behaviours and attitudes of those around us can significantly influence our own actions, even when we aren't consciously aware of it. For example, if we are surrounded by colleagues who regularly drink coffee throughout the day, it's likely we will adopt this habit as well. If we are surrounded by people who share the latest gossip in the lunchroom, chances are we might find ourselves joining in from time to time. These social cues shape our routines and attitudes, creating an environment that subtly steers our behaviour over time. The key takeaway is that if we are placed in an environment surrounded by people who are disengaged, over time, it inevitably reduces our own engagement. Any engaged person will lose engagement when placed in the wrong environment. Therefore, leaders need to know just what is required to create an environment that promotes engagement.

To support positive engagement economics and high performance on teams, there are four important environmental conditions:

- Control
- Expansion
- Culture
- Trust

In the following four chapters, we will explore each of these environmental conditions.

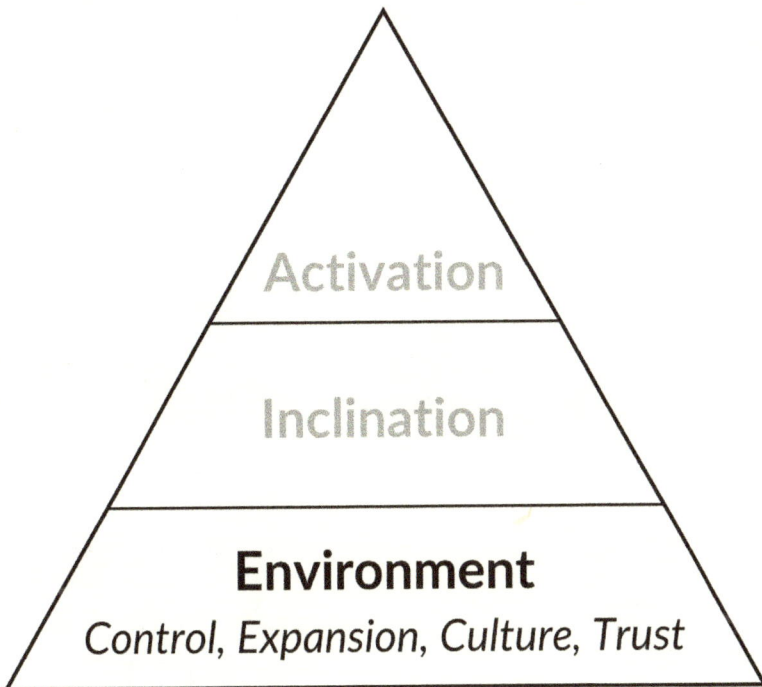

Chapter 5:
Environment—**Control**

Have you ever been subject to the frustrating experience of telling a child not to do something, only for them to do exactly what you told them *not* to do?

"Don't sit on the chair like that; you're going to fall."
"Don't jump on the couch; you're going to hurt yourself."
"Don't push each other; someone is going to get hurt."
"Don't touch that."
"Don't do that."

Yet, they do it anyway.

This behaviour, although easily identified in children, is also very common in adults. If you have ever had a friend or family member tell you what they think you *should do*, it often makes you want to do it less and sometimes makes you want to do the opposite. For example, imagine your spouse or roommate comes to you and says, "You should really clean up the bathroom; it's messy." Even if you had the intention to clean up the bathroom, suddenly your motivation for completing the task is diminished because you are now being *told* to do it. This is what is referred to as **reactance theory**.

REACTANCE THEORY

Reactance theory is the negative motivational reaction to things that threaten or eliminate behavioural freedom. In other words, when people feel like their freedom to feel, think, or behave a certain way is being threatened, they are motivated to resist. This resistance or reactance is an attempt to restore their sense of freedom.

Reactance theory was first introduced by Jack Brehm, PhD in 1966 in an effort to explain why some people are so resistant to social influence, advice, guidelines, or rules. If you think back to a time when it was obvious that someone was trying to persuade you, recall how you felt. For example, think of the aggressive salesperson at the mall kiosk giving you a sales pitch that has been perfected to overcome your every objection. For me, it was this supposedly high-end soap store in the Eaton Centre in Toronto. As I was walking by, the salesperson stopped me by offering a sample of lotion, which, during a Canadian winter, was very much a necessity. I mistakenly took the bait and was roped into listening to her sales pitch for a selection of $100 soaps, lotions, and scrubs from the Dead Sea. She went on about the benefits while scrubbing and moisturizing my hands. As she spoke, she gave me no time to object and only paused after asking me leading questions that made it very difficult to answer without agreeing. "You want healthy skin, don't you?" Well, I mean...who wants *unhealthy* skin? I felt trapped and heavily pressured to do something I didn't want to do (spend $100 on a tiny jar of lotion). During this whole experience, my only motivation was to figure out how to say no and exit the conversation. Before I even knew about reactance theory, I was keenly aware that this salesperson's relentless push to make a sale left me disengaged and eager to escape.

In general, according to reactance theory, we tend to resist attempts at persuasion due to its perceived restriction on our freedom. This process can also occur subconsciously. In a 2009 study by Wellman and Geers, ninety-nine psychology students were separated into groups. The participants were all given placebo pills filled with sucrose. One group was explicitly told that the sucrose pill contained caffeine approximately equal to that of three to four average-sized cups of coffee. They were also told that this pill would enhance their accuracy on tasks, and they were, therefore, expected to perform better. Another group, also given the placebo pills, was given no such expectation of improved accuracy. The participants were assigned a "cross out" accuracy task. They were given photocopied pages of a book on statistics and were told to cross out all the occurrences of the letter "E" that did not fall next to another vowel within the same word.

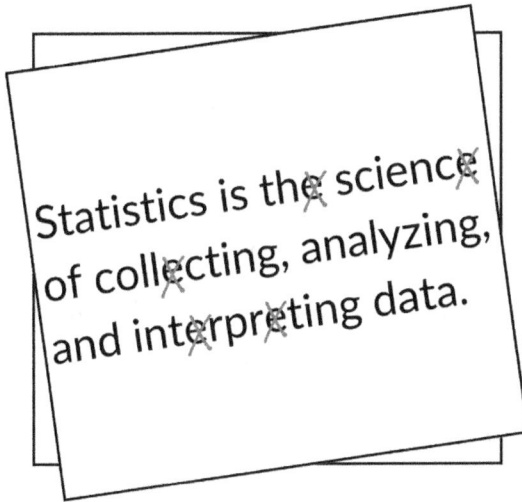

Statistics is the science of collecting, analyzing, and interpreting data.

At first glance, the study's design may suggest that the placebo effect would lead the group that believed they had consumed caffeine to perform better. Instead, the results were influenced by subconscious reactance. The researchers found that the group that was given the *expectation* of improved performance as a result of the pill committed the most errors. The research demonstrates that even subconsciously, when we're given an expectation, we tend to behave in a way that resists the expectation, or we become less motivated to meet that expectation due to the perceived impact on our freedom.[29]

When it comes to participating on teams in the workplace, psychological re-actance has everything to do with our perceived **control**.

Do we have any control over:
- Scheduling our day?
- How we accomplish tasks?
- Where we work?
- What we work on?
- Flexibility in our work hours?
- How we organize things?
- Personalizing our workspace?
- Decision-making processes?
- Career advancement?
- Influencing allocation of resources?
- The learning methods in our learning and training?
- Opportunities to express ideas and concerns?
- Communication channels?

If the answer is no to all the above, and team members are told exactly what to do, when to do it, where to do it, and how to do it, psychological reactance can diminish their motivation and engagement, potentially leading to resistant behaviours. This might look like:

- **Passive resistance**: Deliberately slowing down work or completing tasks with minimal effort.
- **Defiance**: Openly challenging or arguing against instructions.
- **Avoidance**: Procrastinating, ignoring directions, or finding ways to evade tasks.
- **Sabotage**: Intentionally making mistakes or undermining the task's success.
- **Negative attitude**: Expressing frustration, complaining, or creating friction among team members.

That being said, many specific tasks and professions require such precision that strict control must be maintained for safety and success. For example, a surgeon should not be given creative flexibility with regard to operating on patients. There is a controlled process in place to keep people safe. Chefs must follow the recipe for the menu item you ordered and operate the kitchen according to food safety standards. Pilots must keep the plane on course, ensuring a safe and timely landing at your destination.

In work environments with less liability, there is greater flexibility to give people control over their work. This allows more room for creativity in how tasks are approached and helps to overcome psychological reactance. Psychological reactance produces behaviour that is contrary to the desired objective. Therefore, it reduces productivity and performance. Providing the team with control and influence over their work naturally reduces psychological reactance and encourages positive engagement economics. This is also why micromanagement is counterproductive.

CONTROL AND ENGAGEMENT

If you've ever had a micromanager, you would know just how stifling it can be on your overall job satisfaction. Micromanagers closely monitor and control every aspect of their team's tasks, removing any room for creative thinking or autonomy for team members. According to a recruitment organization, micromanagement leads to decreased productivity, less creativity, and an overall negative impact on the work environment.[30] In short, micromanagement eliminates employees' sense of control over their work. Control has a profound effect on engagement.

In the 1970s and 1980s, Edward L. Deci and Richard M. Ryan conducted several influential experiments that laid the foundation for **self-determination theory** (SDT), a framework that explores the psychology of motivation, particularly the factors that foster autonomous engagement. SDT emphasizes the distinction between **intrinsic motivation**—the drive to engage in an activity for the internal satisfaction it provides—and **extrinsic motivation**, where individuals are driven by external rewards or the desire to avoid negative consequences.

Through their experiments, Deci and Ryan discovered that intrinsic motivation leads to better outcomes. It is linked to higher performance, greater creativity, and sustained engagement when compared to extrinsic motivation. One crucial condition they identified in fostering intrinsic motivation was a sense of autonomy—the ability to feel *in control* of one's actions.

The fundamental issue in most workplace environments is that our work is structured on extrinsic motivation. Employees are compensated for their performance and are tasked with working on broader organizational goals that are separate from their personal goals. Unless you have an employee who shows up to work every day for the pure satisfaction of working, intrinsic motivation is limited in the workplace.

I want to focus your attention on an important aspect of SDT which suggests that extrinsic motivation can vary in the degree to which it is autonomous vs. controlled. In their 2005 article, professors and researchers Marylène Gagné and Edward Deci mention a self-determination continuum that describes different types of extrinsic motivation across a range of being more controlled or more self-determined.[31] Therefore, while job descriptions outline specific duties, the degree of autonomy in performing these tasks can vary. This means that although employees often operate in environments driven by extrinsic motivation, the level of control they are given over their responsibilities can significantly impact their engagement. **When responsibilities are highly controlled and rigid, employees tend to experience lower levels of engagement. In contrast, when employees have greater autonomy and freedom in how they approach their tasks, engagement and motivation are significantly enhanced.**

A sense of control not only increases engagement in the task but also encourages efficiency. When employees are given flexibility in how they approach a task, it allows them to experiment with different methods, often leading to faster learning curves and greater innovation. If all aspects of their work are controlled, there is simply no room for experimentation or innovation. Therefore, the goal is not necessarily to achieve intrinsic motivation; it is to increase their control.

You can start in small ways by limiting behaviours that limit perceived control or make employees feel overly managed and take an approach that allows you to manage the outcome but not the process.

STOP
- Providing extremely detailed instructions on how to do tasks
- Requesting to be cc'd on *all* email activity
- Requiring approval for *all* decisions made by the team

START
- Providing details about the desired outcome or result, leaving room for innovation in the process
- Providing constructive feedback instead of instructions

HOW MUCH CONTROL IS TOO MUCH?

One major management concern is that giving employees too much control or autonomy is chaotic and counterproductive or damaging to organizational efficiency. This can be true depending on the circumstances. Giving up complete control in an organization without proper structure is like removing the traffic lights from the roads. Although the drivers may know how to operate their vehicles, there would be chaos while drivers simultaneously try to get to their individual destinations. Every intersection would be a battleground of drivers impatiently competing for the right of way. Any efficiencies in traffic flow would be lost, and urban transportation would descend into a disorganized free-for-all on the roads.

Structure is critical for any system that is effective and efficient. Structure creates a framework to accomplish tasks in a repeatable and effective manner. Traffic lights provide a structure that allows all drivers to use the roads simultaneously in a repeatable and effective manner. Within that system, drivers have control over their vehicles and understand how to operate within the guidelines that traffic lights provide.

The question is, *How do leaders create enough structure that enables them to give their team enough control to be engaged but not too little that the system becomes disorganized and chaotic?* Spotify, a music streaming service, uses a unique method of structuring its teams to achieve this balance.

A Spotify Approach

Spotify identified three areas to focus on striking a balance between structure and freedom:

- Accountability
- Proven routines / repeatability
- Alignment with organizational goals

Spotify's approach includes organizing teams into squads, chapters, and tribes. **Squads** consist of groups of no more than eight people. Each squad is accountable for a particular aspect of the product, such as features, infrastructure, or client application, and is given the authority to decide what to build and how to build it. **Chapters** are comprised of individuals from different squads focused on providing learning and development to support specific functions. **Tribes** are larger groups dedicated to one business area or product. They contain all the squads that are linked together by a chapter.

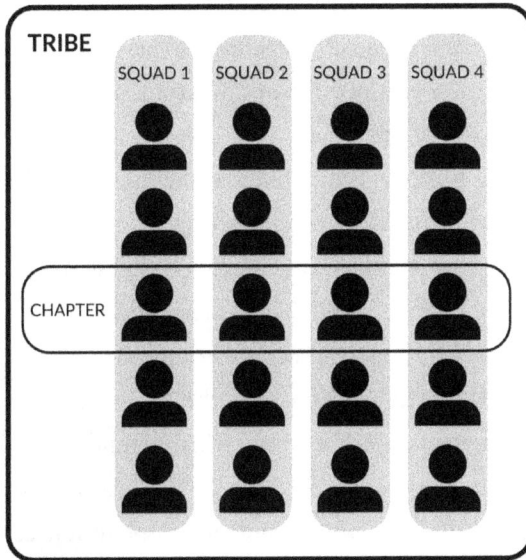

Within the squads, employees have complete control over how they accomplish their work. However, this autonomy is balanced by strict **accountability** for results with measurable objectives, progress, and feedback.

To encourage innovation without losing the benefits of **repeatability**, the chapters function to connect competencies across squads. This allows best practices and expertise to be shared across squads to improve efficiency and eliminate unnecessary or duplication of efforts.

Spotify spends a great deal of time communicating the priorities, product strategies, and organizational objectives of the business so that all tribes have a deep understanding of how their work aligns with the broader direction of the company. By investing in this **alignment**, the company ensures that they are working on the right problems and that squads are collaborating to find the best solution.[32]

When recommending that leaders give their teams more control, the most common objection I hear is a fear that the team will waste resources doing the wrong things. More often than not, however, giving the team more control allows the team to explore efficiencies that they otherwise could not. In fact, I have seen how a lack of control can have employees stuck repeating processes that are wildly *inefficient*. And if you understand unit-level economics (analysis of business profitability at the most basic level), repeating the smallest tasks when inefficient makes scaling unsustainable. For example, imagine you were the owner of a car detailing business. You show your employees how cars should be washed and shined and make it clear that they should follow your instructions exactly. Because they have not been given any control, they do exactly as you say. But the thing is, they know of a better and more efficient way to wash the cars, which would allow them to detail cars in 20% less time, completing eight cars per day instead of six. Continuing to repeat a process, just because it is controlled, does not necessarily make it the most productive approach. Spotify has developed a unique structure that keeps its people focused on the right things while allowing them complete control to find the best way to achieve their objectives. I know it's difficult and often uncomfortable, but giving up *some* control is crucial for engagement and performance. How much? Well, it depends.

GIVING UP "SOME" CONTROL

When trying to identify just how much control you should offer the members of your team, the real answer depends on the nature of the business. Some businesses have the capacity for more creativity. For instance, a marketing agency could give employees the freedom to select which design software to use, how to put together a campaign, and how to communicate with colleagues. A pharmaceutical company, in contrast, would have strict protocols for manufacturing their drugs that call for precise documentation and safety practices.

These are two different organizations on two different ends of the flexibility spectrum.

FLEXIBLE ←————————————→ STRICT

You might find your team on one end of the flexibility spectrum or perhaps somewhere in the middle. Regardless of where your organization and industry land on this spectrum, to increase engagement, **discover where you can increase the number of decisions that your team gets to make.** You can start by looking at the organizational decision categories.

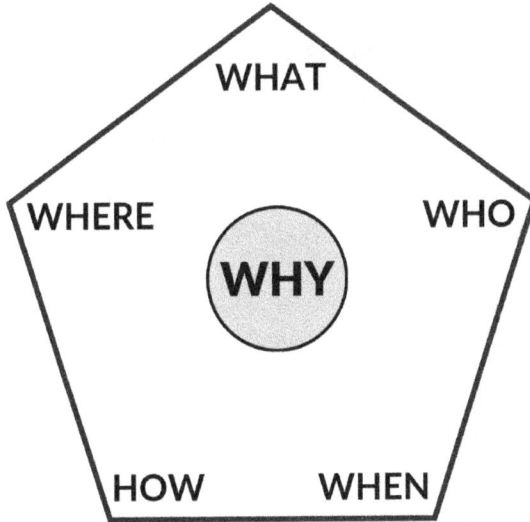

Organizational Decision Categories

WHAT

WHERE   WHY   WHO

HOW   WHEN

At the core of every organization is "why" it exists. The "why" speaks to the overarching vision and mission of the organization. To fulfill that mission, there are considerations or **organizational decision categories** with regard to:

- **What** to do / sell to achieve that vision
- **Who** to involve in achieving that vision
- **When** to implement certain resources to achieve that vision
- **How** to approach achieving that mission
- **Where** to achieve that vision

When analyzing your organization, perhaps there are certain structures in place for *how* things are done. It might not be reasonable to give your team more control over how things are done; however, could you give your team more control over another organizational decision category, such as "when"?

In one company I worked with, which operated in a relatively strict manner on the flexibility spectrum, we realized that team members found it very difficult to maintain work-life balance. This work-life imbalance was increasing their stress and decreasing their engagement. This company had strict procedures that were necessary to keep the end consumer of their products safe. So, we looked at introducing more control with regard to "when." Instead of a strict 8:00 a.m.–4:00 p.m. workday, we introduced the option to choose your own hours. Team members could choose from:

- 7:00 a.m.–3:00 p.m.
- 7:30 a.m.–3:30 p.m.
- 8:00 a.m.–4:00 p.m.
- 8:30 a.m.–4:30 p.m.
- 9:00 a.m.–5:00 p.m.
- 9:30 a.m.–5:30 p.m.

This allowed team members to better manage medical appointments, pick up children after school, and complete a plethora of other tasks that a strict work schedule would simply not accommodate. Leaders simply ensured that team members were appropriately distributed across shifts. Rather than assigning shifts themselves, the leader empowered the team to create the schedule, with the only requirement being that at least one representative from each operational area was present at all times. After this change, employee stress levels were significantly reduced, and as a result, they had more capacity to be more engaged and energized in their daily work.

Toronto Mechanic Shop

There was a mechanic shop in the West End of Toronto that was struggling with a disengaged team, high employee turnover, and difficulty increasing revenue. In an attempt to increase revenue, the owners tried introducing new services—powder coating, bodywork, painting, detailing, and more. This approach was unsuccessful and even resulted in additional costs in recruitment and operations.

It wasn't until the owners were at their wits' end and had run out of ideas that they decided to ask their existing team what they thought could be done to improve the business. To the owners' surprise, the team came up with some really great ideas. The owners decided to take a step back from trying to make all the decisions in every organizational decision category and instead left more decisions up to the people operating the business. With this new control over "how" the business was operating, one of the team members started spending one to two hours per day prospecting, networking, and finding new business—something the owners did not previously allow. After nine months, the shop had an entirely different way of operating—focusing on one service only (automotive repairs) with flexible work hours and continuous improvement projects that were employee-led. After nine months, the shop quadrupled its monthly revenue.

Relinquishing control to your team is not about leaving them to their own devices. It is about sharing the decision-making process to make better decisions as an organization. Striking a balance between leadership control and team autonomy is the best approach.

THE SUPPORTED AUTONOMY SWEET SPOT

Imagine being handed a blank canvas and some paint and being told to come up with an impressive masterpiece. Unless you're a talented artist, the average person would find this extremely overwhelming. It puts immense amounts of pressure on the painter to come up with something that is going to impress without being given any real sense of direction. What colours should I use? Which paintbrushes work best? What should I create? How much time do I have? The painter is left with a series of challenges to address in creating something with absolutely no guidance, direction, or support.

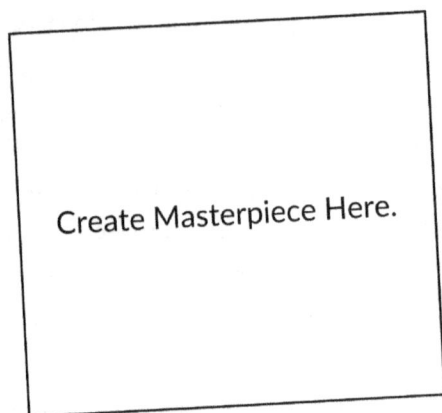

Create Masterpiece Here.

On the other hand, imagine being handed a paint-by-numbers activity and being told to complete it in a week. You look down to see a black and white canvas full of lines and shapes with tiny numbers in each, indicating which colour is meant to be used for each shape. You've been given the set of colours and the brushes that you will need. All the decisions have already been made for you, and therefore, it doesn't necessarily engage your creativity. You simply have to follow the instructions and fill in the shapes.

Image Credit: BestColoringPagesForKids.com

Blank canvas painting and paint-by-numbers are two very different painting experiences, and for the average person, both can be disengaging for different reasons. Blank canvas painting is overwhelming and too unstructured, while paint-by-numbers is too strict and lacks creative freedom.

The real sweet spot for engagement is the Paint Nite concept, also known as guided painting. At a Paint Nite event, a group of painters come together and are given their own blank canvas, brushes, and paint supplies. A professional artist or instructor leads the session, showing everyone how to recreate the featured painting while also encouraging painters to be creative. The instructor is available to help if the painters need it. The event is interactive, as painters chat with one another about their process. In this situation, painters are given a goal (the featured painting), are guided in a general direction, but are also given the freedom to make their own version of the painting. The result is that everyone is engaged in making their own masterpiece guided by the support of the instructor to the extent that they need it. At Paint Nite, participants are given **supported autonomy**.

Here is a photo from my very first Paint Nite.

When seeking a balance between strict and flexible for your team, supported autonomy perfectly describes an environment built for people to thrive. It means that team members are given the adequate amount of support; however, they are also given the autonomy to make key decisions and explore without feeling like everything they are doing is decided for them. They are given enough direction and support to not feel stuck or overwhelmed. They are also not given excessive or strict instruction (micromanagement) that would lead to disengagement. Supported autonomy is the most engaging position to be in on the flexibility spectrum.

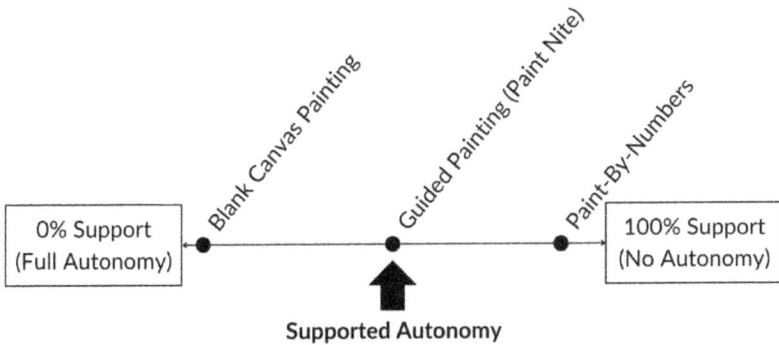

Finding a way to provide the right mix of support and autonomy will prevent micromanagement, reduce reactance, increase creativity, and create lasting engagement. One thing to keep in mind is that different team members might need varying levels of support. Finding the right balance for your team comes with getting to know just how much *control* they need. By satisfying this need, you sustain and support their discretionary effort, enabling better performance and promoting positive engagement economics.

Providing your team with a sense of control is only one aspect of creating an environment that supports engagement. Next, we will explore how employees need room to grow.

Chapter 6:
Environment—**Expansion**

Plants reach for the sky when given enough space to grow.
People do too.
—Unknown

Have you ever heard the **tale of two athletes?**

Athlete #1

From a young age, athlete #1 stood out for his incredible football talent. At six-foot-six and 265 pounds, he was a towering presence on the field. He was strong and had a natural throwing arm that could launch a football farther than anyone in the town had ever seen. His coach called him a "once-in-a-lifetime talent." By his senior year, he had shattered every passing record in the state, amassing over 10,000 career yards. The stadium was always packed with fans eager to watch him play.

Colleges lined up with scholarship offers. He chose to attend a prestigious university, where his talent continued to shine. He led his team to a national title, becoming one of the top prospects in the country. When the NFL draft came, he was the number one pick. The sports world expected greatness.[33]

While his natural talent had carried him through high school and college, the NFL level demanded more. The playbook was complicated, the expectations relentless, and the media scrutiny intense. Training camps revealed weaknesses he never had to face before—his work ethic, his discipline, and his ability to adapt. His rookie season came with many struggles. Coaches questioned his commitment, fans grew impatient, and his once-unshakable confidence wavered.

Year after year, athlete #1 struggled to meet expectations. He was inconsistent on the field, missing key plays and failing to develop as a leader. The talent was still there, but the drive was not. By his third season, the team cut him, abandoning their hopes for their once-promising star. Soon after, he was out of the league altogether.[34]

Athlete #2

Athlete #2 began his career as the backup quarterback on the junior varsity team in high school. At first, he was not even good enough to be a starting player for this team, which had not scored a touchdown all year. It was only once the starting quarterback was injured that athlete #2 achieved the starting position. He worked extremely hard and strived to be noticed by college coaches, creating highlight tapes and sending them to schools of interest.[35]

At the college level, athlete #2 spent two years as a backup quarterback, struggling to get playing time. He was extremely frustrated and anxious and even went to a sports psychologist for help. He also worked with the assistant athletic director every week to work on his confidence and maximize his performance. With hard work and consistency, he was able to improve his results.[36]

Athlete #2 was drafted to the NFL as a sixth-round draft pick; however, he had to work hard to prove himself and earn the trust of his teammates and coaches. Athlete #2 embraced the challenges and continued to focus and work hard in order to increase his performance, recognizing that there was a lot of room for growth and expansion.

The Moral of the Story

Athlete #1 is the story of a player considered to be a "draft bust" (a highly selected draftee who does not meet expectations). It is the story of unfulfilled potential and the harsh reality that talent alone is not enough to survive at the highest level.

Athlete #2 is Tom Brady, the seven-time Super Bowl-winning quarterback, often considered one of the greatest in NFL history, with multiple MVP awards.

The difference? **Expansion.**

Expansion is the ability for team members in an environment to grow. An environment that offers expansion offers team members room for growth and development. An environment that does not offer expansion will eventually leave team members feeling stuck or stagnant with limitations on what they can learn or accomplish. A truly engaged team will have a natural desire to grow and to see progress. If there is no room for expansion, your team will outgrow your organization and seek a new place to grow. Or worse, they stay and stop growing.

EXPANSION AND ENGAGEMENT

Most of us know what it feels like to be stuck. In fact, a Google search of "feeling stuck" delivers thousands of results on "what to do when feeling stuck in life." A quick review of the articles on the first page of search results reveals timeless wisdom: You might have outgrown your current situation, and it is time to reassess your needs and wants. Feeling stuck is the opposite of feeling engaged in something. When we are engaged in our work, there tends to be some level of curiosity as a result of having room to grow and learn. When there is no space for expansion, your employees may start looking elsewhere.

Building HR from the Ground Up

I once consulted with an HR manager at a construction company in Toronto who had an unconventional career path. Before stepping into HR, she had a background in education. A fast learner, she quickly outgrew her role in that field and began searching for new opportunities.

That's when she came across a small construction company looking for an HR manager. She applied, and during the interview, she made such a strong impression on the CEO that he offered her the job on the spot—something that rarely happened. Excited about the opportunity, she drafted her resignation letter and informed her current manager about her decision to leave.

To her surprise, her manager countered with a matching salary and benefits package, hoping to keep her on board. The offer made her pause. At her current job, she had stability and knew exactly what to expect. The thought of stepping into the unknown made her second-guess her decision. In the end, she chose to stay.

But a higher salary and better benefits didn't solve the real issue—she still felt stuck. Within six months, regret set in, and she resumed her job search. She reached out to the construction company again, only to find that they were still looking for an HR manager. This time, she didn't hesitate. She joined the team.

As a small company, they had few established HR policies or procedures—she had to build everything from the ground up. When I asked if she found it overwhelming to create an HR department from scratch, she simply smiled and said, "I am excited by the challenge. There is so much room to grow, and they give me the autonomy to explore and learn. The work is hard but in a good way."

An environment that offers **expansion**—in other words, the space for employees to learn and grow in their roles—keeps team members engaged. They get to explore new heights and new possibilities, finding new ways to contribute to the team. As they grow, they bring fresh perspectives, deeper knowledge, and greater expertise that ultimately benefit the entire team and the organization as a whole. It begins with creating learning and development opportunities.

BENEFITS OF LEARNING AND DEVELOPMENT INITIATIVES FOR EMPLOYEES

According to LinkedIn Learning, 94% of employees would stay at a company longer if the company invested in their learning and development. There is a strong connection between employee retention and the availability of learning opportunities to allow them to **expand** their professional achievements. Part of engagement is knowing that your current efforts are leading somewhere gratifying. An organization that offers expansion allows its team members to feel like they are advancing in their careers—as if their efforts and learnings are leading them somewhere better.

With learning and development initiatives, although upfront costs can be expensive, there are several engagement and business outcomes that provide a return on investment in performance and profitability:

- **Improved Performance and Productivity**: It is no secret that a team member with well-developed skills and knowledge will have the ability to perform better. Continuous improvement allows team members to learn about the latest industry standards, giving them the ability to produce higher-quality work more efficiently.

- **Innovation**: Continuous learning encourages team members to be creative and look at situations from different perspectives with new knowledge. Exposure to new ideas and skills can inspire employees to bring new ideas and innovation to their roles, creating a competitive edge for the team.

- **Better Talent Attraction**: Recruiting, hiring, and onboarding new employees is expensive. Investing in learning and development initiatives makes talent attraction more cost-effective and efficient by enhancing employer branding, increasing internal promotions, and reducing turnover, ultimately attracting high-quality candidates who seek growth opportunities while minimizing external hiring costs.

- **Reduced Turnover and Improved Talent Retention**: Replacing an employee can cost **50% to 200% of their annual salary**, while companies with high retention rates experience a **22% increase in overall profitability**. By keeping top talent, organizations save on hiring expenses, maintain productivity, and preserve institutional knowledge, leading to stronger long-term performance.[37]

- **Supported Succession Planning**: Learning and development initiatives are a strategic way to create a succession funnel. Constantly training team members to operate with the knowledge and skills as would be required in the successive position creates a qualified pool of candidates to choose from.

By virtue of the team engagement need for expansion, there are several proven positive outcomes that stem from learning and development initiatives, as outlined above. However, one of the long-standing challenges for organizations is justifying the spending on training and development due to the difficulty of measuring the exact impact on performance and profitability. The good thing is that there are several formal methods for evaluating training programs, the most popular being the Kirkpatrick Model.

The Kirkpatrick Model is a widely accepted standard framework for evaluating training programs and was developed by Donald Kirkpatrick in the 1950s. Donald Kirkpatrick was Professor Emeritus at the University of Wisconsin and a past president of the American Society for Training and Development. His model uses four levels of evaluation:

- **(Level 1) Reaction**: refers to the participants' initial opinions of the training program itself.
- **(Level 2) Learning**: describes whether the learning objectives were achieved and whether participants have the knowledge the training program intended to deliver.
- **(Level 3) Behaviour**: measures the degree to which participants' behaviours change as a result of the training—basically whether the knowledge and skills from the training are then applied on the job.
- **(Level 4) Results**: measures organizational return on investment such as reduced cost, improved quality and efficiency, increased productivity, employee retention, or increased sales.

The Kirkpatrick Model is a useful tool to help organizations evaluate the success of learning and development initiatives. Each level comes with increasing complexity of measurement; however, it provides a methodology, tools, and best practices to support your analysis of training effectiveness and to prove the return on investment of expansion initiatives.

An environment that offers **expansion** through learning and development opportunities is an important part of generating positive engagement economics. However, expansion doesn't happen without proper planning.

EXPANSION PLANNING

To avoid a scenario where team members feel "stuck" or outgrow their roles, it's important to build an environment with expansion in mind. Ask yourself, Once team members become proficient in their role, what new skills could they learn that would contribute to the success of the team? You might consider implementing a standard expansion plan, something more personalized, or just including some general expansion initiatives.

Standard Expansion Plan

One way to do it is to have a standardized expansion plan for the role, which includes predetermined and standardized advancement levels. We see this in the apprenticeship structure. An apprenticeship is a structured training program that combines paid on-the-job experience with classroom instruction, allowing team members to develop specialized skills under the guidance of experienced professionals. Apprentices gradually take on more responsibilities as they work through course materials and complete assessments, typically over one to five years, depending on the trade or industry. Upon completion, they receive a certification, which qualifies them for higher wages and career advancement.

For example, a mechanic apprentice generally follows these steps:

1. Start their position and register as an apprentice.
2. Complete classroom training and complete exam.
3. Do apprentice level 1 on-the-job training.
4. Complete classroom training and complete exam.
5. Do apprentice level 2 on-the-job training.
6. Complete classroom training and complete exam.
7. Do apprentice level 3 on-the-job training.
8. Complete specified on-the-job hours.
9. Write and pass certification exam.
10. Obtain full certification.

Implementing a standardized growth structure for all team members contributes to engagement by providing a clear roadmap for their learning journey. This structure allows team members to see a well-defined path towards achieving specific levels of expertise and success. By creating a similar framework within your organization, you can ensure that employees understand exactly what they need to learn, give them clear milestones to track their progress, and engage them in their continuous development.

However, if the nature of your organization is not a good fit for a standardized expansion plan, you might consider a personalized expansion plan.

Personalized Expansion Plan

A personalized expansion plan offers a tailored approach in which each team member has a unique path for advancement. This works best if your team is made up of a variety of positions that require different skill sets and would have very different learning journeys.

For example, think of Pixar Animation Studios. You've likely seen a Pixar film such as *Finding Nemo, Toy Story,* or *Monsters, Inc.* Creating animated films requires a range of roles and specialized skills such as animators, storyboard artists, software developers, voice actors, musicians, marketing and distribution teams, and more. Such a range of roles demands more personalized training.

A personalized expansion plan tailors the growth journey to each employee's unique skills, career goals, and areas of interest. This method is highly effective at engaging team members because they get to co-create this plan. They get to choose their learning objectives and have a say in the courses, experiences, and mentorship that align with their aspirations. As an added bonus, the more involved someone is in designing a plan, the more committed they are to its execution. This personalized approach helps employees feel more engaged in their development because they have a direct role in shaping their learning paths.

Among other learning initiatives, Pixar offers a collection of in-house courses through its Pixar University. Pixar University offers a variety of courses to help people develop in their careers but also offers many optional classes. Some (screenplay writing, drawing, and sculpting) are directly related to the business, and some (Pilates and yoga) are not. This allows the team to continue to learn and expand, pursue both their professional and personal interests, and reinforce a mindset of continuous improvement.[38]

To create a personalized expansion plan, you must first identify the way in which each team member wants to expand. Which skills do they want to grow? What experience do they want to have? What are they interested in? What are their goals?

If you're starting from scratch and need to find out this information, you can host one-on-one interviews where your employees can candidly express their goals. In these situations, you might notice your team member expressing some reservations about sharing their goals with you. If that's the case, try to reassure them that if there is a way you can help them achieve their goals, you'd like to try. But don't pressure them to share these aspirations. Lean into co-creation and ask questions like:

- What adjustments do you think we could try that would help you achieve your goals?
- What are some things you've always wanted to learn about that you think would be beneficial to your career?

Work together to first come up with broad ideas and then narrow it down into a realistic plan for their expansion. The plan would outline your commitment as a leader to providing expansion opportunities as well as the employee's commitment to actively pursuing and completing them.

Be sure to book a follow-up meeting during the interview with your team member. Many leaders fall short of the commitments they make to their team because they get busy. Nothing destroys your credibility more than over-promising and under-delivering. Make sure to follow up and deliver updates on any progress. Once the personalized expansion plan is in place, you'll also want to book regular check-in meetings and create feedback loops to ensure progress is tracked and adjustments are made where needed.

General Expansion Initiatives

Outside of a standardized or personalized expansion plan, there are many other less formal or structured ways to create space for expansion and growth. Here are some other initiatives to consider:

- **Provide a Budget for Professional Development**: For example, offer each team member a $500 budget to be spent on professional development of their choosing, which could include courses, workshops, conferences, or other learning experiences.
- **Offer Subscriptions to E-Learning Platforms**: Many online learning platforms (such as Udemy, LinkedIn Learning, and

Coursera) offer access to entire suites of courses that cover a wide range of professional development topics.

- **Host Lunch and Learns**: A Lunch and Learn is a short training session usually held over lunch where learners come together and have the ability to learn while sharing insights and experiences. A Lunch and Learn can be formal (facilitated) or informal (open discussion). By definition, a Lunch and Learn should include food!
  - ○ Note: Be cautious when implementing Lunch and Learn Programs. Be careful not to make team members feel like they need to sacrifice their lunch hour for this. Consider offering alternative incentives, such as time in lieu or perhaps some really great free food.
- **Implement a Mentorship Program**: Pair team members together to encourage them to learn from one another. Establish mentor-mentee relationships that foster knowledge sharing, career growth, and leadership development.
- **Book Workshops with External Subject Matter Experts**: Bring in industry experts to provide specialized training on relevant skills, new technologies, or emerging trends that will help employees stay ahead in their field.
- **Take Your Team to Industry Events**: Networking at conferences, trade shows, and seminars allows employees to gain industry insights, build professional relationships, and bring fresh ideas back to the organization.
- **Allow for Innovation Time**: Giving your employees free time to work on innovative projects of their choice offers them a way to explore new skills that also benefit the organization.
- **Offer Tuition Reimbursement Programs**: Provide financial assistance for employees to pursue higher education or specialized courses.

- **Create Cross-Training Opportunities**: Allow employees to learn from different departments to build new skills and enhance versatility.
- **Build a Company Library**: Encourage reading by stocking a variety of professional development books that are made available to employees to borrow.

Whether you take a standardized, personalized, or general approach, providing opportunities for expansion is a powerful driver of employee engagement. Engaged employees are good for business. The initiatives above range in cost, making it possible to find options that align with your company's budget. However, the cost of offering nothing is far greater—leading to high turnover, disengagement, and a stagnant workforce. Investing in employee expansion not only enhances skills and innovation but also strengthens retention. When employees see that their organization values their growth and is committed to the future, they are more likely to envision themselves as part of that future.

While the future is essential, the day-to-day team environment is also vital for engagement. This is where culture comes in.

Chapter 7:
Environment—**Culture**

I used to believe that culture was "soft," and had little bearing on our bottom line. What I believe today is that our culture has everything to do with our bottom line, now and into the future.
—Vern Dosch, technology leader and retired CEO of National Information Solutions Cooperative

Before his start in leadership positions and as president of a graphics and print effects company called ASL Print FX, Charlie MacLean started his career at the globally renowned brand Coca-Cola. In an interview, he shared with me that on his very first day, he recalls walking in the doors, excited about his new job but not sure what to expect. "Almost immediately, the passion of the people hit me so hard. I said, 'Wow...these people are really excited about this soft drink.'"

Everybody at Coca-Cola was living and breathing a culture of positivity. Together, they promoted the brand, worked as a team, and truly lived the brand message. For Charlie, this environment was unlike any other work environment he had witnessed in the past. He was accustomed to people simply showing up to work just to fulfill their duties, get their tasks done, and go home. At Coca-Cola, however, the underlying message was that either you drink the cola, find a passion for the product, and get on board with the culture, or be left behind. What Charlie remembers most is the contagiousness of the culture. He realized that if he had stepped into a culture where all the employees were disgruntled and unhappy about the brand, he would have simply said, "Well, I guess that's just how things work around here."

Culture, whether positive or negative, is contagious. Like a virus, it finds its way into contact with all the team members of an organization until they catch the bug. Some people seem to have a stronger immunity at first, but over time, the cultural contagion will always affect every team member. **Team culture is powerful because it is a discernible force that has the ability to transform attitudes, productivity, and performance.** Because it is so influential and contagious, it is crucial that organizations take an active role in shaping what type of "cultural virus" is circulating through their team.

WHAT IS ORGANIZATIONAL CULTURE?

Organizational culture describes the attitudes and behaviours of employees or team members within an organization, which directly impacts all other aspects of the organization, including engagement.

Cultural Initiation

Derek, a young professional just starting his career, landed a job as a sales representative for a large multinational company. As part of his training, he was paired with a senior account manager for job shadowing and mentorship. The senior account manager demonstrated the process of prospecting, consultation, quotation, and customer onboarding. Derek, who was eager and excited to make his first commission and apply the training, spotted a great prospective opportunity for a new customer. Derek shared this with his mentor (the senior account manager), asking for advice on the best way to approach the situation. To his surprise, his mentor listed several reasons why the opportunity was *not* worthwhile and essentially convinced Derek not to approach the prospect. Two weeks later, Derek found out his "mentor" had approached the account behind his back and secured the business along with the commission that came with it. Devastated, Derek asked his "mentor" what happened and was told, "That's just business." This was Derek's introduction to a workplace culture of competition and deceit. Against his better nature, Derek learned very quickly not to assist his colleagues and to keep information close to his chest.

IMPACTS AND OUTCOMES OF POOR ORGANIZATIONAL CULTURE

Poor organizational culture can have many obvious effects on team engagement and performance:

- A culture of competition and deceit eliminates collaboration.
- A culture of low effort hinders productivity.
- A culture of fear impedes innovation.
- A culture of resentment creates sabotage.
- A culture of indifference disrupts organizational effectiveness.
- A culture of disempowerment breeds defeatism.

There are also several hidden outcomes of poor organizational culture, including organizational silence, equity theory, learned helplessness, and defensive working.

Organizational Silence

Organizational silence refers to the phenomenon where individuals refrain from speaking up or taking action in response to significant problems that face an organization.[39] Although there may be serious consequences for the team or the organization, poor organizational culture can be the reason that team members choose not to speak up.

Nurses in hospitals are notoriously busy, overworked, and underappreciated. Organizational silence might exist in a hospital setting; for example, a nurse might notice a colleague taking a shortcut that could have potential consequences for a patient, but the nurse chooses not to confront the colleague because they know how difficult it is to get all their work done. In this case, nonconfrontation is culturally acceptable because all the nurses are feeling overworked and underappreciated. To get their work done, they might take shortcuts and rely on each other's silence.

Equity Theory

Equity theory suggests that employee motivation at work is driven largely by their perception of fairness. According to Gartner, equity theory in action looks like "employees creating a mental ledger of the inputs and outputs of their job and then using this ledger to compare the ratio of their inputs and outputs to others."[40] Inputs include things like effort, commitment, overtime work hours, and exceeding expectations. Outputs include things like salary, benefits, recognition, and awards. If an employee perceives that the culture of the organization does not fairly reward inputs with outputs, they will adjust their inputs. For example, if one employee who does not put in much effort is often praised or given salary increases, other employees begin to recognize the inequity, which reduces their motivation to continue to put in the same level of input. In an inequitable culture with the absence of meritocracy and fair recognition, comparison and resentment will be heightened, which ultimately reduces engagement.

Learned Helplessness

Learned helplessness is the condition in which a person has a sense of power-lessness after having faced a negative situation or failure multiple times. With learned helplessness, individuals stop trying to change their circumstances even when they have the ability to do so. In organizational culture, this normally manifests in two ways. The first is a result of **bureaucracy**.

When I worked for a multinational packaging company in the health care division, I remember feeling overwhelmed by the number of procedures we had to abide by. If I recall, there were over seventy standard operating procedures that directly applied to me, in addition to customer-specific procedures developed over time at customer request. The customer-specific procedures were distributed as paper documents, and with the number of customers we had, these paper documents amounted to two six-inch heavy binders on our desks. Just looking up a procedure was a challenge as you had to flip through hundreds of pages. Of course, I asked why these documents could not be made accessible as digital files. Multiple colleagues shared that there were past attempts at tackling this project, but not a single attempt was approved by management for compliance reasons that were unclear. Over time, people stopped trying to change the circumstances. People stopped trying to make improvements and efficiencies because they believed it wouldn't go anywhere anyway. Many heavily regulated industries such as health care / pharmaceuticals, food and agriculture, energy, and finance often feel they have their hands tied due to regulations or legislation. Over time, the construction of approval procedures, reviews, audits, metrics, decision chains, recurring meetings, and other management processes to satisfy regulations are used as the very reasons innovation or change cannot happen. The repeated reminders of limitations and being told things can't be done fosters a culture of learned helplessness, discouraging team members from even attempting to make change.

The second way in which learned helplessness often manifests in an organization is through **negativity**. In these circumstances, suggestions and ideas are met with negative responses such as "That will never work," "I wouldn't even bother," or "That will never get approved." This is a form of psychological punishment for behaviour that challenges the status quo. It directly discourages team members from even thinking about putting forth ideas for change or improvement. Even when conditions change, and an idea could succeed, employees affected by learned helplessness will remain convinced that failure is inevitable.

Battling learned helplessness within organizational culture requires challenging all assumptions and rewarding behaviour that pushes boundaries and questions the status quo. This means fostering an environment where innovation is encouraged and failures are seen as learning opportunities, which we will discuss later in this chapter.

Defensive Working

Although defensiveness is a natural psychological response in the face of feedback or criticism, poor organizational culture amplifies it. Poor organizational culture hinders constructive dialogue. One key characteristic of poor organizational culture is an "us vs. them" or "me vs. them" attitude where self-preservation outweighs collaboration. In these instances, employees engage in behaviours that help them avoid punishment but do not necessarily contribute to the best interests of the team. For example, an employee might notice a mistake in a document made by a colleague but, instead of correcting it, deliberately forwards it as-is, knowing it will reflect poorly on their colleague. If the document is sent out to a client, it could have negative consequences for the entire organization. As a result, defensive working can lead to sabotaging behaviours. In some cases, when mistakes occur and managers provide feedback, employees may deflect blame, deny accountability, or respond with counter-criticism. This not only impedes personal growth but also prevents the organization from addressing the root cause of the problem.

SHIFTING ORGANIZATIONAL CULTURE FOR ENGAGEMENT

Your people come first, and if you treat them right, they'll treat the customers right. —Herb Kelleher, founder of Southwest Airlines

We've seen how poor culture can erode performance. It creates the very behaviours that impede team success. Positive organizational culture, on the other hand, not only creates engaged, high-performing team members but also contributes to profitability, even in times of economic hardship. Culture can be the very thing that saves the day when strategy and planning fail or when unforeseen circumstances like a global pandemic arise. Nobody, including Southwest Airlines, saw COVID-19 coming.

Southwest Airlines, Where Culture Is First Class

The collapse of demand for flights during the COVID-19 pandemic in 2020 put many airlines out of business; however, Southwest Airlines was not one of them. Southwest Airlines is a strong example of a company that prioritizes team culture and has reaped the rewards tremendously.

In 2017, Kristin Robertson, CEO of Brio Leadership, attended the Southwest Airlines Culture Connection, a half-day event that showcased the company's methods of strengthening, reinforcing, and maintaining its strong positive culture. At the time, the company boasted stats such as:

- 4% voluntary turnover
- Forty-four consecutive years of profitability
- #1 lowest number of customer complaints
- 85% employees reported being proud to work for Southwest
- No layoffs, no furloughs ever

Kristin was excited to learn about the inner workings of how to maintain such a positive company culture. Here are some of the key lessons:

1. **Evolve Your Culture**: Since its formation in 1967, Southwest Airlines has had a sense of its cultural values; however, it wasn't until the 2000s that it formalized its workplace culture by explicitly identifying its values as "The Southwest Way." Today, it is very clear how those values translate into their daily operations.[41]

2. **Equip Leaders, Regardless of What Position They Have**: Leaders are recognized at all levels of the organization hierarchy, not just at the top. Anyone, regardless of their position, who demonstrates leadership qualities has the opportunity to attend leadership training where they learn about the company's managerial best practices. These leaders are further encouraged to take care of their team by being given the authority to spend money to take care of team members, such as sending flowers in the event of a death in one's family.

- **Empower and Appreciate Employees**: Southwest Airlines has a strong sense of recognition and appreciation within its team culture. Any compliments received by customers are forwarded directly to the employee and their manager so they can be appreciated for contributing to customer satisfaction. Southwest Airlines also has a peer-to-peer recognition system where team members can send other team members points for their efforts. These points can be exchanged for items in a catalogue that the company provides.

Let's look at another example of an organization where positive organizational culture contributes to high-performing teams.

Culture and Performance with SWAT

The highest-performing unit in the police service is the Tactical and Rescue Unit, better known as Special Weapons and Tactics, or SWAT for short. SWAT units are highly trained and equipped to resolve high-risk situations such as hostage circumstances, barricaded persons, violent robberies, or other situations involving deadly weapons.

After speaking to an active Canadian operator working as part of the Tactical and Rescue Unit, it became clear that within the Tactical Unit, the operators are separated into teams. In this service, each of the teams happens to have significant team cultural differences. Those cultural differences impact the way in which the teams perform. Although all teams operate according to organizational standards and the overall police service mission, performance-based metrics such as mission success and training statistics differ slightly between teams. All teams demonstrate high performance; however, the teams with the highest mission success and best training statistics have key positive cultural characteristics. Those include high emotional intelligence, a collaborative (not competitive) mindset, and a high sense of personal accountability.

Digging deeper, I found that the culture of each SWAT team is largely affected by the leadership approach of the team leader. Operators working in the Tactical and Rescue Unit find themselves in high-pressure situations in which they must act with precision in order to achieve their objectives. Team leaders are responsible for making key decisions in those high-pressure situations. Team leaders on the highest-performing teams who have successfully instilled high emotional intelligence, a collaborative (not competitive) mindset, and a high sense of personal accountability on their teams also exemplify these characteristics and more. Operators report that team leaders who create constructive learning environments that encourage growth while challenging team members to give their best effort at all times contribute to a positive working environment, even in a highly specialized and dangerous job.

Positive team culture creates positive engagement economics. When looking to build positive team culture for a more engaged and high-performing team, how do you know if you have the right recipe? What are the key ingredients of a culture of engagement?

WHAT CONTRIBUTES TO A CULTURE OF ENGAGEMENT?

Organizational culture directly impacts team engagement. The amount of discretionary effort employees choose to give, in large part, has to do with how the organizational culture dictates behaviours and attitudes. When looking at examples of positive organizational culture, it becomes clear that there are certain characteristics of the culture that support employee engagement. To avoid the hidden outcomes of poor culture (organizational silence, equity theory, learned helplessness, and defensive working), certain values must be maintained by the organizational culture.

After analyzing top examples of team cultures that foster engagement and high performance, five key characteristics consistently stood out. Evidently, these same traits were absent in teams with poor culture. They were:

- Respect
- Failure safety
- Recognition
- Fairness
- Empathy and understanding

Respect

Picture this: You're in a meeting with your team discussing a mistake that was made. One of your teammates throws you under the bus, calling you incompetent in front of the entire team. None of your other teammates stand up for you, and you leave the meeting angry about your teammate's disrespect.

You're in a bad mood for the rest of the day. Now you feel the need to distance yourself from the team to focus only on your required tasks, speaking only when spoken to, or worse, you're dead set on finding a way to get back at your teammate. The perceived disrespect has disrupted your engagement with the team, shifting your focus from the team's performance to navigating the interpersonal dynamics ahead.

In Maslow's Hierarchy of Needs, esteem is the fourth level after physiological needs, safety needs, and love and belonging. Our esteem needs are fulfilled through respect. We must feel respected by our team members to feel engaged and to want to contribute meaningfully to the team. A culture of respect creates a foundation for engagement to be built upon. Without respect, or in the instance of disrespect, a natural psychological response is resentment, a barrier to engagement.

The Mental Health Commission of Canada published a list of thirteen psychosocial factors that support mental health in the workplace. One of those factors is "civility and respect." It describes a workplace where employees are respectful and considerate in their interactions with one another and with customers, clients, and the public. Organizations that have cultivated a culture of respect generally have a more positive atmosphere where people feel comfortable in the work environment, allowing them to focus on contributing to the team. A culture of incivility and disrespect generally leads to a greater number of conflicts and job withdrawal. Disrespect can also escalate from frustration to intimidation to harassment and even violence. Beyond the damage to engagement, disrespect and incivility exposes the organization to more grievances and legal risks, which are costly in morale, time, and legal or investigative fees.[42]

A culture of respect sets a baseline that prevents the escalation of negative behaviours. Team members feel valued and operate under a common understanding that they all play a role in accomplishing the organizational goals, regardless of their ethnic background, language, religion, working style, gender, or any other physical or psychological differences. With that understanding, the team members treat one another with respect, creating an environment where engagement can thrive.

Failure Safety

Fail early, fail often, but always fail forward. —John C. Maxwell

Early in my career, I was working for a large manufacturing organization. In my first year, I distinctly remember a mistake I made while preparing forms for job dockets. As I was printing out these forms, I thought to myself, *If I print the forms double-sided, we can save some paper.* So, I proceeded to double-side the forms, slip them into the job docket envelope, and send them off for production. At this organization, mistakes were reported in non-compliance reports (NCRs) that outlined your name, the job docket associated with the mistake, a description of the issue, notes from the manager, and corrective actions. The number of NCRs issued to an individual was seen as a direct reflection of their performance and played a role in performance evaluations. NCRs were also made visible to the entire team because they were posted on a bulletin board inside the plant where everyone could see. This created a culture of fear around receiving NCRs. I recall instances where team members would say, "Please don't give me an NCR!" and rush to resolve issues on their own, even in situations where involving a manager would have been the better approach.

I came in to work one morning, and to my surprise, I had been written up in eleven NCRs. I was devastated. Eleven NCRs! Most people might only get a few in an entire year. Overnight, I had eleven! Turns out, I had been written up for every job docket where I had printed the forms double-sided. I was devastated because my intention was to save paper. However, I still had to go through the NCR process and meet with my manager to discuss the root cause of the issue, write out corrective actions, and sign off on each of the eleven NCRs. From that day forward, I felt scared to make mistakes and didn't want to step outside of the lines. I experienced first-hand how this culture of fear around mistakes would encourage people to follow procedures yet prevent people from thinking outside of the box.

Failure is life's best teacher. Think of the moments in your life where you thought to yourself, *Well, I'll never make that mistake again.* Those moments likely became turning points for changes in behaviour and opinion. In my professional life, beyond the eleven NCRs, I have made plenty of mistakes. The silver lining is that each one turned out to be a valuable lesson on what I should do differently the next time.

Many organizations view failure as something to be avoided at all costs; however, punishing or stigmatizing failure is very harmful to the organization. Placing high-pressure expectations on team members, demanding that they get things done right the first time, will ensure that they follow procedures accurately; however, it discourages them from trying new solutions that might create improvements. Team members who are afraid of the repercussions of failing refrain from voicing concerns, sharing ideas, or highlighting potential problems.[43] As a result, although procedures are followed correctly, the most effective or innovative path forward may be overlooked.

Consider a scenario where your team is working on a project with a fast-approaching deadline. The project has several flaws that should be addressed as soon as possible. The team members recognize the issues and believe there could be a better way to approach the project. However, they hesitate to raise concerns because they operate in a failure-unsafe culture where failure is punished. Instead of proposing a new approach, the team members follow the existing process out of fear of repercussions for deviating from the standard practice. As a result, the project moves forward, consuming more time, budget, and effort than necessary, only to encounter significant setbacks down the line. These setbacks could have been avoided if your team felt comfortable enough to voice their constructive input and outside-the-box ideas earlier.

Post-It Notes, A Successful Failure

Did you know Post-it Notes were born out of failure?

In 1968, Dr. Spencer Silver, a researcher at 3M, was working on increasing the strength of adhesives for materials to be used in the aerospace industry. His efforts failed tremendously, and instead of creating strong adhesives, he ended up creating an adhesive so weak that it could be removed easily without leaving any residue behind. Due to its failed status, this project was put on the shelf, where it stayed for six years.[44] After six years, a colleague of Silver, Art Fry, discovered a use for Silver's failure. Every week, while practicing with his church choir, he would use small scraps of paper to mark the hymns they were going to sing. But the scrap papers constantly fell out of the book. He needed a bookmark that would stay in place.[45] Silver's adhesive was the perfect fit, so together, Fry and Silver worked on a prototype using the only scrap paper available at 3M—yellow. Once the product was complete, they not only found themselves using them as bookmarks but also using them as a way to leave notes around the office. Fry said, "It's a whole new way to communicate."[46]

3M launched this product to the market under the name Press'n Peel in 1977. Press'n Peel, originally the result of Dr. Spencer Silver's failed project, had an unsuccessful market launch, unfortunately, marking another failure for 3M. Press'n Peel was removed from the shelves. Two years later, in 1979, 3M decided to try again, but this time with a new approach. This time, they launched a free sample campaign, sending free samples to businesses all over Boise, Idaho. This approach proved to be a massive success. Ninety percent of businesses that received a free sample placed an order. From there, sales grew exponentially. Today, Post-it Notes are an international success. To what do they owe this success? 3M's culture of failure safety allowed their employees to research, explore, fail, and try again in order to come up with creative solutions that ultimately led to success.

How to Create a Culture of Failure Safety

If your team seems to be lacking innovation, it may be time to foster a culture that embraces failure as part of the growth process. As a leader, there are three key actions you can take to encourage this shift.

1. **Encourage Idea Sharing**: Leaders should actively encourage team members to share ideas and experiment with new solutions for improvement. The underlying message should be that all ideas are welcome—there are no bad ideas, only opportunities to learn. Whether the idea succeeds or fails, it is essential that team members feel valued for their initiative and contribution.

2. **Talk About Your Failures**: Leaders often feel pressure to maintain an image of perfection in front of their teams. However, one of the most powerful ways to remove the stigma around failure is by sharing their own experiences. By openly discussing their setbacks and the lessons learned, leaders can set the tone for a culture of failure safety, transparency, and growth, encouraging team members to do the same.[47]

3. **Focus on and Celebrate the Lessons Learned**: Remove the emphasis on the failure itself and focus on the lesson learned and how to apply that to future situations. When people fail, it's natural for them to feel a sense of disappointment. Rather than reiterating what they already know and feel, leaders should focus on celebrating team members for their efforts and the valuable insights gained from trying something new, even when the outcome isn't as expected. This might look like an insight bulletin board where team members are

thanked or recognized for the lessons that were created for the team or a round of applause in a team huddle. The more positive reinforcement team members receive for making an effort in innovation or improvement, the more that behaviour is encouraged.

Embracing more opportunities for risk-taking by creating a culture of **failure safety** greatly increases the likelihood of **success**.

Recognition

A few weeks ago, I went to the mall to shop for new pants. As I opened the doors to the mall entrance, I glanced over my shoulder to see if there was anyone behind me to ensure I held the door open long enough for them to walk through. While no one was immediately behind me, there was a middle-aged man who was about fifteen feet away. I decided to take the extra time to wait for him to get to the door. He looked up, saw that I was waiting for him, and sped up his walk just slightly to show his intention to walk through my door. As he got closer, I smiled and said, "Take your time." As he walked through the door that I held open for him, I looked at him, expecting him to acknowledge what I had just done with a, "Thank you," or even just a smile. That "Thank you," or smile never came. I felt the sting of bitterness. I even thought about muttering, "You're welcome," so he might recognize the courtesy I had just paid him. Instead, I just thought to myself, *Why didn't he recognize that I didn't have to sit there and wait for him to get to the door?* I took extra time to pay him a kindness, and it wasn't even appreciated. What I did notice at that moment was how quickly the enthusiasm for going the extra mile (discretionary effort) could be diminished with a lack of **recognition**.

Recognition may seem small; however, it is a very impactful way to support employee engagement. Its absence has significant impacts on employee engagement and lost productivity. If someone consistently goes the extra mile, offering high discretionary effort, but is never recognized for their efforts, they inevitably begin to wonder...*Is it worth it*? Over time, these employees who feel undervalued begin to withdraw. They may still show up but are less likely to bring energy, ideas, or initiative. Eventually, their commitment fades. According to Gallup, employees who do not feel adequately recognized are twice as likely to say they'll quit in the next year.[48]

Recognition is often overlooked; however, in our personal lives, we know all too well how impactful recognition can be on engagement. For example, think of the invisible labour that is divided between partners in a relationship or a family (or what I call our "teams at home"). In many relationships and families, invisible labour goes unnoticed, leaving the others unaware of how much effort is truly being invested. For instance, one partner might take on the invisible labour of organizing family gatherings. Hence, they might spend a lot of time and effort coordinating with others, purchasing and organizing supplies, making phone calls, sending messages, and ensuring everyone is kept informed. The result of all this invisible labour is well-organized family events. Now imagine if all that effort consistently went unrecognized. Nobody shared their appreciation. Over time, the organizer will begin to wonder...*Is it worth it*? Even worse, what if instead of recognizing and appreciating the effort, a family member criticizes the outcome of the other partner's efforts? Perhaps they make comments such as, "It would have been better if you did it this way," or "Why didn't you do...?" Such comments, devoid of recognition, will leave that partner not only feeling unappreciated but resentful and questioning why they go above and beyond in the first place. Over time, that engagement slowly disappears. They might scale back their discretionary effort or might even opt out of planning family gatherings altogether.

Consider this instead:

- What if every time you held open a door for someone, you were met with a smile and a "Thank you so much!"?

- What if your contributions to your family and relationships were met with a "Wow, that was amazing! Thank you so much. I really appreciate all that you do!"?
- What if your contributions at your job were met with a "Wow, your contributions really made a difference. Thank you so much!"?

How much more likely are you to *continue* going above and beyond now?

> *A person who feels appreciated will always do more than what is expected.* —Amy Rees Anderson, entrepreneur, angel investor, and philanthropist

Elevating Culture with Recognition at O.C. Tanner

According to Josh Bersin, founder at Bersin by Deloitte, companies with a recognition-rich culture have a 31% lower voluntary turnover rate.[49]

O.C. Tanner is a company that specializes in employee recognition and workplace culture. They support companies in building recognition programs by offering software, tools, expertise, and awards. They share many client success stories of workplace cultures that have been transformed by the inclusion of a recognition program. One such client, an insurance company with over 40,000 employees in twenty-five different countries, wanted to establish itself as the employer of choice, demonstrating high engagement and retention. To improve employee experience and achieve these goals, they partnered with O.C. Tanner to take their recognition program from good to best-in-class.

This project was championed by the executive leaders and created a consistent global experience for all employees. From O.C. Tanner's article, the key features of the program included:

- A points-based program with peer-to-peer recognition
- Expanded award offerings (over 6,000 awards to choose from)
- Social recognition tools so employees could comment and like one another's recognition
- A new Yearbook solution to recognize years of service
- Localized solutions for global locations, with a program in their local language and local catalogues and awards that resonate with their employees. [50]

Each aspect of their recognition program was designed to amplify recognition moments and also to create meaningful ways for employees to support each other.

Often, however, intention and impact are not the same. Many employers implement recognition programs with good intentions but fail to have a meaningful impact because they do not measure the result nor gather feedback. Far too often, I've seen HR-led "Gold Star" programs that are launched with good intentions but miss the mark due to a lack of clarity and transparency. Recognition is typically shared in company publications or internal communications based on criteria that aren't well understood by the team. Without clear guidelines or broader involvement, these efforts usually feel disconnected and ineffective. What's more, peer-to-peer recognition is often limited or entirely overlooked—missing a key opportunity to build a culture of shared appreciation.

In partnership with O.C. Tanner, this particular insurance company sent out regular surveys to gather data, comments, and suggestions for improvement for the program. They've taken this feedback and made improvements to the program that created noteworthy results. Most notably:

- Satisfaction with recognition was up twenty points from their previous program.

- Participation numbers have exceeded global benchmarks by double digits for over three years (and counting).
- Employees who send and receive more recognition had a higher probability of being a Net Promoter and lower odds of attrition, saving the company $10-$15 million per year in attrition costs.[51]

Pro Tip: Criticism > Recognition = Disengagement

One thing I've learned about employee recognition is that it needs to be loud and proud. Most organizations have a habit of being loud about the mistakes of their employees but quiet about recognition. For example, if an employee makes a mistake in a client document, they might be written up, called into the manager's office for a meeting, or become the reason that a company-wide reminder to "Make sure you double-check things before sending them to clients" goes out. High-performing employees generally feel very badly about making mistakes, so multiple layers of discipline to address mistakes can feel disproportionate and may ultimately do more harm than good.

On the other hand, when an employee goes above and beyond, perhaps preventing a costly mistake or stepping in at a critical moment, I've seen companies respond with little more than a quick thank you email or a casual message on Microsoft Teams, like "Thanks so much, Janet!" While well-intentioned, this kind of recognition is often far too quiet compared to the significance of the contribution—especially when you consider how loudly mistakes are treated in comparison.

The point is that **if criticism feels louder than recognition, it contributes to disengagement**.

Fairness

Imagine you were the coach of a soccer team. During practice, you split the team in half for a scrimmage match. What do you think would happen if you split the teams unfairly? Let's say you split the teams unevenly, giving one team the advantage of having extra players in addition to placing all the best players on that team. The end result is a scrimmage match with eleven of your top players vs. five of your developing players. Recognizing the unfair disadvantage, the team of five doesn't focus on winning; they focus on survival. Their strategy is to defend against the team of eleven for as long as possible. During the match, the team of eleven continuously scores on the team of five. The team of five that was burdened with an unfair disadvantage is feeling frustrated and resentful and begins to wonder why they are even participating in this match. However, if you had split the players fairly into two teams of eight with skill levels evenly matched, both teams would have been able to focus on how best to use their strengths to succeed. Both teams would be engaged and motivated to win.

To create a culture of engagement, a sense of fairness must be established. When things are unbalanced or unfair, team members are too focused on the imbalance to engage in the work.

For example, consider two team members who have the same job title and do the exact same amount of work. If those two team members have a vast gap in their wages, the team member who is getting paid significantly less will find it difficult to feel engaged and motivated because the conditions in which they operate are unfair. This might not just look like a difference in wages; it could also be:

- Unfair workloads or tasks
- Unfair expectations
- Unfair treatment
- Unfair access to opportunities

- Unfair disciplinary practices
- Unfair application of policies or rules
- Unfair performance evaluations
- Unfair distribution of rewards or bonuses

Recall **equity theory**, whereby employees are motivated by a sense of fairness in the workplace, comparing the ratio of their inputs and outputs to others. If an employee perceives that the culture of the organization does not fairly reward inputs with outputs, they will adjust their inputs.

A workplace environment and culture without fairness creates inconsistency. Inconsistency creates an environment of uncertainty. An uncertain environment often creates a survival mode response in team members. Instead of focusing on their contributions, team members focus on how to navigate the unfair playing field and whether or not it is worth participating in the first place.

Unfairness is highly distracting. A team culture which allows and promotes unfairness breeds disengagement.

Empathy and Understanding

Seek first to understand, then to be understood.—Stephen R. Covey

At the beginning of my consulting career, I remembered a very important lesson. Although I had learned several consulting and coaching techniques and had witnessed many leaders use different styles to support their team, I recall working with one individual who was struggling with motivation. In our first meeting, I pulled out all the tools that I would normally use, including worksheets and assessments, in order to map her satisfaction and dissatisfaction in different areas of her life, including her job, mental health, physical health, hobbies, and personal life. In that meeting, she shared with me that she had experienced a difficult separation from the father of her children. Without him, she felt lost with all the new responsibilities she had acquired in addition to having lost her individuality in the busyness of being a mother. I had seen this exact situation before and was familiar with how it was affecting her motivation. Thinking I knew better, I jumped to providing solutions and action plans that I was certain would work for her. I told her we would reconnect after she had some time to implement one of the solutions we discussed to see where she was at. She agreed, and we scheduled a follow-up call. However, to my surprise, she missed our next scheduled meeting. I followed up with emails to check in to see if she was okay, but I heard nothing from her for weeks. Months later, she told me that she felt overwhelmed in our session and was really looking for support in her healing from the separation. She was not ready to implement the solutions that I rushed to give her. My mistake was skipping over empathy and understanding and moving straight to the solution. I realized then that sometimes the right solution is found in empathy. Looking back, I recognized that my assumption—that I could solve her problem—prevented me from asking what type of support she was looking for. Failing to ask and acting on assumptions about her needs critically impacted our ability to work together. All I could think was *Well, I'll never make that mistake again.* Since then, in every consultation or coaching session—whether with teams or individuals—I have made it a priority to understand their unique situation, the type of support they're seeking, and what they expect from our work together. Empathy and understanding come first. People want to feel heard and understood.

After interviewing leaders who have successfully cultivated engaged and high-performing teams, two words consistently emerged in discussions about how they built their culture. Those words were **empathy** and **understanding.**

Ace

Understanding what someone is really trying to do, is the best way to get things done. —Lauren DeSouza, CEO, Ace

Lauren DeSouza, the CEO and co-founder of a tech company called Ace, says, "At risk of sounding like a broken record, I believe culture is really about empathy."[52] In our interview, she explained that most issues, whether between coworkers or with customers, can be resolved by having empathy and making an effort to understand the other person's perspective.

The Ace approach to building a culture of empathy consists of setting a foundation of understanding from the beginning. Lauren says, "When starting to work with others, each person has chosen to be a part of the team for a different reason. It may be to gain more experience, to advance their career, or build skills that will allow them to start their own business in the future."[53]

Understanding these individual drivers is key to being able to create an environment for meaningful engagement. Using Stephen Covey's guiding principle to *first understand, then be understood*, it is important to ask questions such as: What would you like to see out of this relationship? Taking the time to understand your team members' objectives and then clearly communicating your own as a leader fosters a collaborative and empathetic environment where all parties can work together as a team to accomplish those goals. This approach increases engagement, creates mutually beneficial relationships, and establishes a foundation of understanding that cultivates a culture of empathy.

By fostering a culture of empathy and understanding, we transform transactional relationships into genuine human connections, where mutual understanding works to prevent issues caused by misaligned expectations.

At Ace, culture is also at the forefront of their hiring decisions. Recognizing that there are so many talented people out there with technical skills, degrees, and certifications, deciding between candidates often comes down to whether they will fit the culture.

Lauren shares that she is frequently faced with the challenge of choosing between two candidates with the following characteristics:

- Candidate A has ten years of experience and possesses exceptional technical skills. However, they exhibit a reluctance to learn and grow, likely due to their strong belief in their expertise.
- Candidate B has about half the experience but demonstrates remarkable passion, a strong desire for continuous improvement, and a willingness to participate.

Ace always chooses Candidate B because Candidate B aligns with the culture that they have built. Ace has been able to build a highly engaged and high-performing team by shaping the team culture. Lauren intentionally selects team members who fit the culture, and she leads with empathy. Lauren mentions, "As a leader, I impact the culture by leading with empathy and understanding so that I can identify the things that people truly care about and how best to invest in them." This approach has worked exceptionally well for Ace.

Pro Tip: Points of Caution

In cultivating empathy and understanding, there are a few things to be cautious of.

Be Cautious of Empty Gestures

In an effort to understand employees and make them feel heard, many organizations turn to surveys. While the intention may be genuine, these efforts quickly lose credibility if no meaningful action follows. When survey results are collected but not acknowledged, or worse, never acted upon, employees may perceive the gesture as disingenuous or performative. Rather than feeling heard, it creates the impression of a superficial commitment to listening. Over time, employees continue to feel unheard, misunderstood, and that their input holds little weight, ultimately undermining engagement.

There's No "Winning" the Argument

Let's take a moment to reflect on our home teams. Many of us have experienced the frustration of a disagreement where we feel unheard. Perhaps it's with a family member, a partner, or even a close friend. You're going back and forth, trying to make your point, but the other person can't seem to understand your perspective. Overall, the conversation is unproductive because they aren't hearing what you're trying to communicate. The problem is that we often enter disagreements trying to prove why we're right or to "win" the argument. In reality, trying to prove that you are right rarely leads to a positive outcome. There's no real "winning" in that scenario. A true win-win is achieved by creating an environment where both parties feel genuinely heard and understood.

Until you understand the other person's strengths, weaknesses, and perspectives, you will always be working against one another instead of as a team.

Chapter 8:
Environment—**Trust**

Without trust, we don't truly collaborate; we merely coordinate or, at best, cooperate. It is trust that transforms a group of people into a team.

—Stephen Covey

When you look at the pit crews in professional NASCAR racing, you'll immediately notice the speed and precision with which they operate. In the 2024 NASCAR Cup Series Campaign, there were 213 pit stops where four tires were changed, and 89 of those pit stops took ten seconds or less. The fastest pit stop time was 8.88 seconds.[54] While this time is extremely impressive, having the fastest pit stop time does not win races. The consistency of pit stops wins races. Depending on the track, a race will generally have two to six scheduled stops. During those pit stops, not only are the tires changed, but the crew may also refuel, clean the windshield, and make adjustments to things like tire pressure and suspension settings. The point is that the actions taken during a pit stop are critical to the success and safety of the driver. To accomplish such critical tasks in a matter of seconds requires a lot of trust.

Becky Greiner, a contributor at *The Daily Downforce*, says, "Each NASCAR pit crew has specific roles and responsibilities, and each role must be perfectly in sync with the rest of the team to send the driver on their way as soon as possible without compromising safety."[55]

In a pit crew, there are tire changers, a tire carrier, a jackman (who jacks or raises the car), and a fueler. Each team member must **trust** that everyone will execute their tasks with accuracy and on time. There is no time to double-check each other's work, no time to micromanage, and no time to doubt one another. Small mistakes have the potential for catastrophic consequences. However, without trust, these pit crews would not be able to perform at their best.

AN ENVIRONMENT WITHOUT TRUST

Let's go back to grade school. Do you recall stressful situations working with other students? Most group work is difficult for students because it is often a low-trust environment. If you don't have haunting memories like I do and are not already familiar with the process, student groups would typically divide the assignment and work on a subsection of the assignment independently. Afterward, they would combine all the sections and submit the final project.

The process is rarely smooth. Each of the students may have different working styles, skills, and even different levels of commitment in the course. Anxiety builds when the committed students doubt whether their less-committed team members will deliver on their responsibilities. There could be a series of missed milestones, a lack of responsiveness, and nothing to show for promises made to the group. In this situation, eventually the committed students will give up on trying to engage the other students. Since their grades are on the line, those committed students begrudgingly end up doing all the work to compensate for their uncommitted and untrustworthy peers. To streamline this frustrating process, the uncommitted group members are likely to be dropped from communications (since they don't contribute anyway). At the end of the process, everyone is frustrated. If you were lucky enough to have project groups with peers who were trustworthy and committed, then you're lucky to have had a positive experience that was not poisoned with doubt. The result of a low-trust team environment, high in doubt, is disengagement, duplication of work, and barriers to communication.

A low-trust environment breeds doubt. Doubt impedes engagement and hinders team performance.

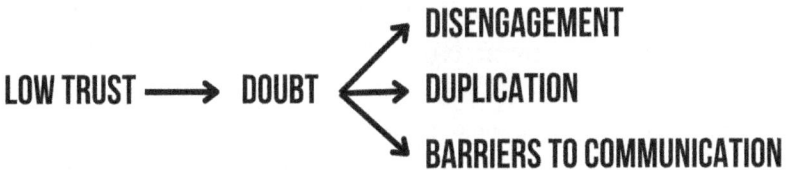

LOW TRUST ⟶ DOUBT ⟷ 　DISENGAGEMENT
　　　　　　　　　　　　　DUPLICATION
　　　　　　　　　　　　　BARRIERS TO COMMUNICATION

When members of a group show a lack of commitment and trustworthiness, it causes committed team members to feel disengaged, wondering why they should work so hard if others are not. The committed group members often find themselves duplicating the work of other team members just to get things done, which creates tension and drives wedges between team members. This usually leads to fragmented communication, with side conversations and private group chats forming as a way to circumvent the lack of collaboration. A low-trust environment breeds doubt on any team, whether it's our teams at work, our teams at school, or even our teams at home.

A Low-Trust Environment at Home

A lack of trust in your personal life might also be affecting your teams on the home front. Perhaps it's the dishes in the sink, something your partner or a family member always leaves behind without washing. You ask your partner / family member to put the dishes in the dishwasher and turn it on before bed. They say, "Yeah, I will." The next morning, you wake up, and the dirty dishes are still there. Frustrated, you ask your partner / family member a second time to take care of the dishes.

When they fail to complete the task again and again, falling short of their word, you can't help but feel frustrated and annoyed with them. What's worse is you no longer feel like you can trust your partner / family member to get things done, so you just do it yourself. As you're completing their task, you might start to feel resentful towards them. Your tone sharpens with frustration when you're communicating with them. You wonder why you should have to put in more effort than they do. You begin to feel disengaged.

Over time, consistently failing to follow through on commitments creates a low-trust environment, and that lack of trust will spark the beginnings of disengagement in those relationships.

TRUST-PERFORMANCE MATRIX

The Navy SEALs are the United States Navy's primary special operations force. They are highly trained to operate in a variety of environments, including sea, air, and land. Within the Navy SEALs is a highly renowned and elite special operations unit called SEAL Team Six. They are considered the "elite within the elite," with hand-selected Navy SEALs for the most specialized missions. Simon Sinek, author and inspirational speaker, was curious as to what characteristics were truly required to be part of what is considered to be the highest-performing organization in the world. In an interview with the

Navy SEALs, Sinek asked how such a high-performing organization selects the members of SEAL Team Six. He shared that in order to answer his question, the Navy SEALs drew him a matrix, the Trust-Performance Matrix.[56]

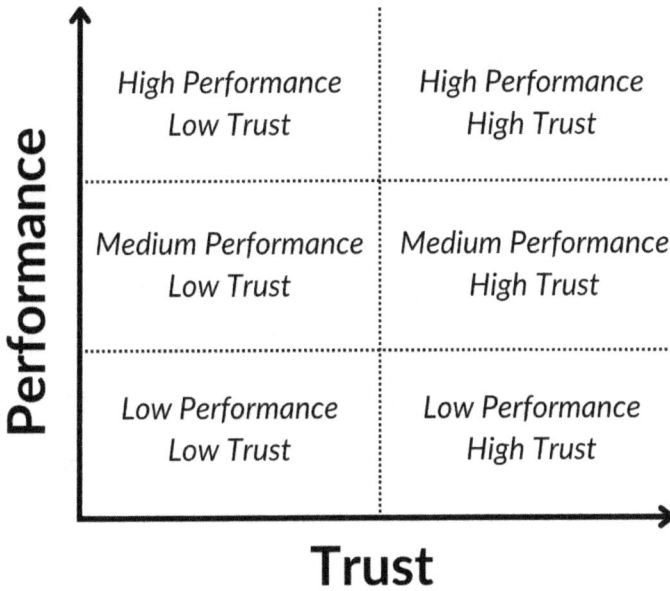

In the matrix, there were two axes: performance and trust. Performance refers to the team member's performance on the battlefield, including their skills and results. Trust is whether or not the team member has integrity. As you might expect, the Navy SEALs told Sinek that, of course, nobody wants a low performer with low trust, and, of course, everyone wants a high performer with high trust. However, many people fall somewhere in the middle. The SEALs identified interesting characteristics about those in the middle of the spectrum. They said that a high performer with low trust is a toxic leader and a toxic team member. Although this person might perform well, they will have a negative impact on the team around them. The Navy SEALs recognize that a lack of trust has the ability to undermine a team's success by damaging the team environment. Therefore, the Navy SEALs would rather select a medium performer with high trust or sometimes even a low performer with high trust over a high performer with low trust. **The highest-performing organization in the world values trust before performance.**[57]

THE RESULTS OF TRUST

Evident in high-performing organizations, like NASCAR pit crews or SEAL Team Six, an environment of trust makes effective collaboration possible. When a team collaborates effectively, there can be engagement, efficiency, and communication.

TRUST ⟶ COLLABORATION ⟷ ENGAGEMENT
EFFICIENCY
COMMUNICATION

Due to its impact on collaboration, trust has an impact on the cost of results. In a low-trust environment, results cost more. Hidden costs are found in direct labour costs as a result of duplication of work and the reduction in efficiency when communication is strained or when team members cannot be trusted to fulfill their responsibilities. In high-trust communication, people give each other the benefit of the doubt. Mistakes are understood or forgiven because trust is strong and intent is clear. In contrast, in low-trust communication, team members show up as skeptics, looking for even the smallest errors as proof of bad intent. This lack of trust creates strained interactions, defensiveness and contributes to disengagement.[58] The impact of low trust on engagement also leads to indirect costs from a reduction in overall productivity.

If a NASCAR pit crew operated in a low-trust environment, pit stops of 8.8 seconds could not be achieved consistently. If SEAL Team Six operated in a low-trust environment, there would be dangerous consequences. Lives could be lost, and the success of missions would be put at serious risk.

A high-trust environment reduces the costs of results. By facilitating collaboration, team members work more efficiently and effectively, taking their contribution seriously and knowing they can rely on others to do the same. An environment with high trust encourages engagement, therefore also increasing discretionary effort and productivity for the team.

Even large companies like Netflix specifically focus on building trust as a way to boost performance.

Netflix and ~~Chill~~ Trust

Netflix, the global streaming service, is on a mission to entertain the world, "thrilling audiences everywhere," as they put it. In order to do that, they mention "creating an environment where talented people can thrive—lifting ourselves, each other, and our audiences higher and higher."[59]

One of their core principles is to build "The Dream Team," which means seeking the high performers—*"people who are great at what they do and even better at working together."*

After looking further into how Netflix builds their dream team, it was interesting that they specifically mentioned that they model their team after a professional sports team, not a family. Many corporate leaders will tout the notion of being a family at work. Netflix points out two reasons why your team at work is different from your family. First, families are about unconditional love. You're not at work to develop unconditional love for people who are being paid to fulfill a position. Second, families can often be dysfunctional.

Using the professional sports team mode, Netflix focuses on performance. On a professional sports team, take soccer, for instance, where each player has expertise that allows them to fulfill the needs of their position. For the team to be successful, they must each successfully play their own position while also collaborating with their teammates in other positions to maintain possession of the ball and ultimately score. No one teammate can play all positions. Successful teams develop mutual trust, where each player is confident that their teammates will be there to support them when it counts.

The same is true for Netflix. They focus on creating high-performing teams built upon a foundation of trust. They create trust by encouraging values such as selflessness, candor, and inclusion. They define each value as follows:

- **Selflessness**: Helping others succeed.
- **Candor**: Giving and receiving feedback, sharing mistakes and lessons learned.
- **Inclusion**: Recognizing your biases and working to counteract them so that everyone (no matter their culture, identity, or background) can do their best work.

On any team, an environment of trust creates mutual confidence that contributes to engagement. When employees trust one another, they are more willing to support their teammates and are more invested in their work. Trust reduces internal friction so that less time is spent managing conflict or second-guessing the intentions of others.

Busy leaders like Dr. Deena Kara Shaffer certainly do not have the time nor wish to spend their time second-guessing their team's intentions.

Trusting in the 99%

In an interview with Dr. Deena Kara Shaffer, author, public figure in education, and CEO of Awakened Learning, I asked about how she has been able to engage learners and engage her team. For her, relationships are at the centre of her leadership and education approach. She said, "I would never start a meeting with action items before asking how people are doing and what's top of heart and mind. There's no point in sharing a strategy with a learner who is absolutely stressed, rushing, racing in. They need a moment to settle and know that they can connect with you." Dr. Deena believes that the best engagement strategies are deeply relational and are based on trust. While working as a director at a Canadian university, Dr. Deena shares how she was able to support her team effectively and maintain engagement. She said, "If someone needed to work from home because they had a sick kid, the answer was yes. If their partner worked night shifts and they needed flexibility outside the formal hybrid arrangement, the answer was yes. Does it make your life easier? Does it make your work more doable? Then the answer is yes. Some people would say, 'Aren't you worried about being taken advantage of?' I'm just not going to spend my minutes worrying about that. The alternative—being hard-nosed and creating more rigidity? No thanks. I'm going to **trust in 99%** of people's good nature and say yes. And sometimes, just that trust alone makes people want to live up to being worthy of it. **What I do know is that the best managers are those who give their team the space and trust to do the work**."

The question is, *How* do we build more trust within our teams?

Pro Tip: Build Trust with Reliability

Building more trust on your team requires a consistent demonstration of reliability from leaders and team members. The more consistent members of a team are, the greater the team's confidence will be in reliability, and the stronger the overall sense of trust will be within the group. In contrast, inconsistency within the team can quickly erode trust.

When evaluating whether actions are fostering a low-trust or high-trust environment, consider the presence of reliability in key areas:

- Is there reliability in keeping promises and following through on commitments?
- Is there reliability in communication?
- Is there reliability for deadlines?
- Is there reliability in performance?
- Is there reliability in attendance?
- Is there reliability in integrity?
- Is there reliability for taking responsibility for actions?
- Is there reliability in maintaining confidentiality?
- Is there reliability in demonstrating loyalty and standing by your team?

Building a high-trust environment involves demonstrating reliability and holding others accountable to the same standard.

Trust is the final environmental need for engaged teams. When **trust** is paired with a sense of **control**, the ability to **expand,** and positive team **culture**, all the needs for an environment that promotes engagement and high performance are satisfied.

Environmental Key Takeaways: We Don't Always Choose Our Team

Our environment is the foundation for our engagement needs. Team members and humans, in general, adapt to the environment in which they are placed. Therefore, an environment that promotes disengagement will only create more disengagement. In contrast, an environment that fulfills the team member's engagement needs will naturally encourage team members to invest more fully, strengthening commitment and performance.

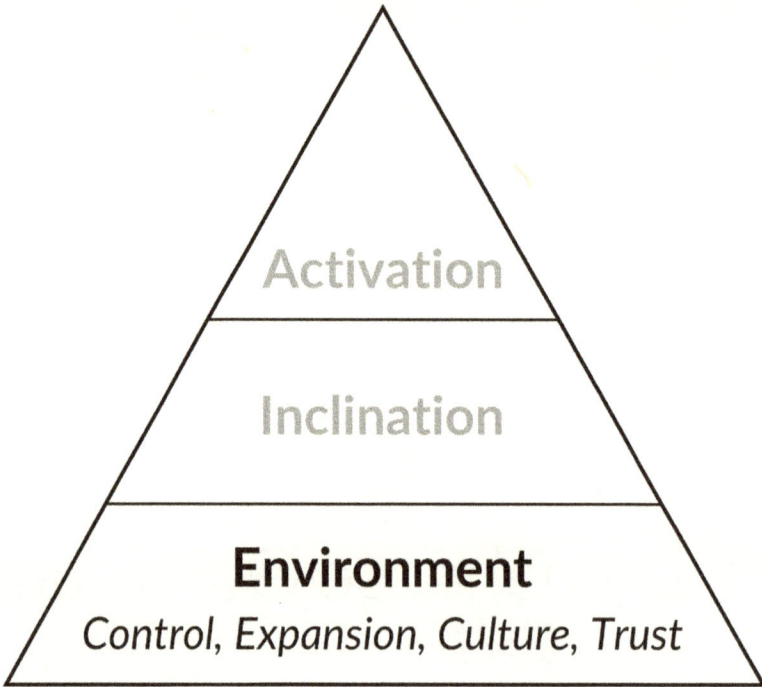

While it may seem like something that is difficult to control, leaders do have the ability to choose the environment in which the team operates. This is done by defining what is acceptable and what is unacceptable. It may be as simple as intervening when you spot unproductive behaviour or as complex as building a work structure that is flexible and fits their needs for control. Either way, employees, especially when they first join the team, are seeking to understand the boundaries of their team environment.

Think about what happens when a new employee joins the team and is looking to understand how things work. Every day, this new employee shows up to work early to demonstrate their punctuality and sense of responsibility. However, several coworkers show up to work late every day without an excuse. The manager notices their lateness but says nothing. The new employee begins to wonder if being late is *acceptable* and whether punctuality is really that important to the organization. Although things can be difficult at times, the new employee also prioritizes respect and kindness in the workplace. However, they notice that several coworkers have angry outbursts when things don't go their way, and the whole team can hear their screaming and shouting. The manager notices these outbursts but says nothing. The new employee begins to wonder if angry outbursts are *acceptable* and whether respect and kindness are valued by the organization. When the leader fails to make it clear that negative behaviours are unacceptable, a poisonous thought starts its inception on your team. That thought is...**Well, if they can do it, why can't I?**

When leaders make it clear which behaviours are acceptable and unacceptable, team members gain an understanding of the boundaries of their environment.

For example, imagine if your team was in a brainstorming meeting. An employee decides to put forth an idea. A coworker immediately shoots it down and condescendingly says, "That doesn't make sense. It will never work." You, as the leader, call out the comment and say, "Instead of making condescending comments, please respond in ways that build on one another's ideas and create solutions." At that moment, the entire team is made aware that condescending comments are *unacceptable*. The thought that now permeates the team is...**If they can't do it, I better make sure that I don't either.**

The definition of acceptable and unacceptable behaviours, in other words, the boundaries of the environment, is the responsibility of the leader.

As a leader, while you may not always be able to choose your team, you have the power to define the environment in which they operate. Keeping in mind the team's need for a sense of control, the ability to expand, a positive culture, and high trust, leaders can truly create an environment that promotes engagement.

Once the environmental needs are satisfied, we can ascend to the next layer in the Hierarchy of Team Engagement Needs to unlock deeper levels of engagement. That next level is **inclination**.

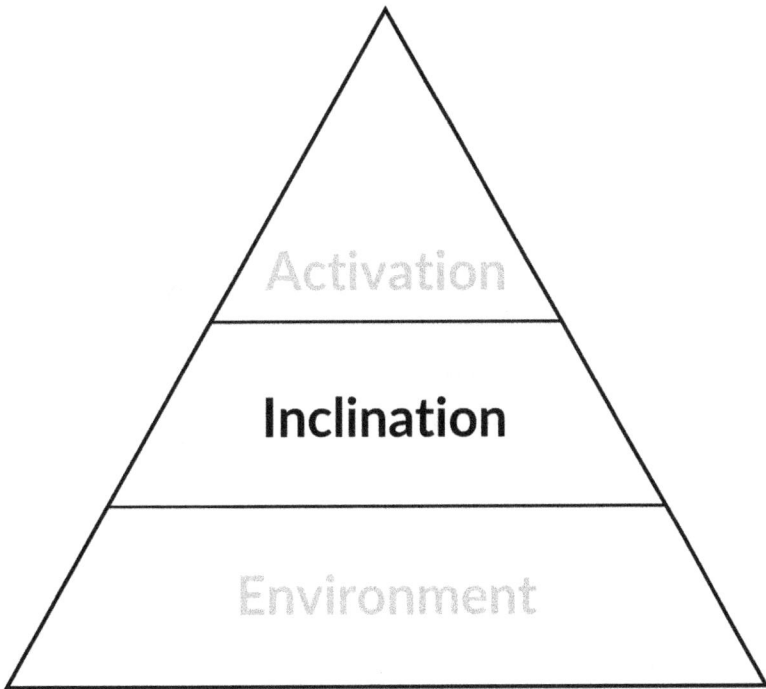

Chapter 9: Inclination

Are you someone who enjoys filing your taxes every year? I would imagine that this is a tedious and frustrating process for you like it is for most of us. Perhaps you've opted to do it yourself, or maybe you pay to get it done for you. Either way, if filing taxes is a dreadful process for you, it is safe to say that you don't feel inclined to start a career as a tax accountant. For those of you who enjoy navigating the tax process and have become successful tax accountants, I am happy for you.

In order to be engaged, over and above our environment, we need to be inclined towards the goal or the work that we're involved with.

Someone who prefers to be more creative might find themselves disengaged if they had to analyze financial data all day. Someone who enjoys organized processes and procedures would be more engaged in a structured project as opposed to one that seems chaotic. Take Oprah for example.

Before Oprah Winfrey was the OPRAH that we all know, she worked as a news anchor and reporter at a news station in Baltimore. Oprah shares that she felt misplaced and was never truly comfortable with her seat on the 6:00

p.m. news. She recalls feeling exhausted and having to drag herself to work every day. She was even told that she was unfit to be a news reporter because she couldn't keep her own emotions out of the stories.

With her strained relationship with her work, one day, in 1978, Oprah was demoted to the role of co-host of a talk show called *People Are Talking*. She got to interview the man who invented soft-serve ice cream, and what first seemed to be a setback in her career suddenly created a shift. She writes: "My entire body told me this is what I was supposed to do."[60] All of a sudden, Oprah found herself engaged in the work she was doing, all because she discovered that she had an **inclination** for this type of work. She writes: "That day, my 'job' ended, and my calling began." Today, we all recognize Oprah's success and the iconic moment when she famously declared, "You get a car, and you get a car!" to her studio audience. Oprah's inclination enabled her to tap into engagement and propelled her career to new heights.

Tapping into inclination could mean the difference between a mediocre career and a highly engaging and fulfilling one.

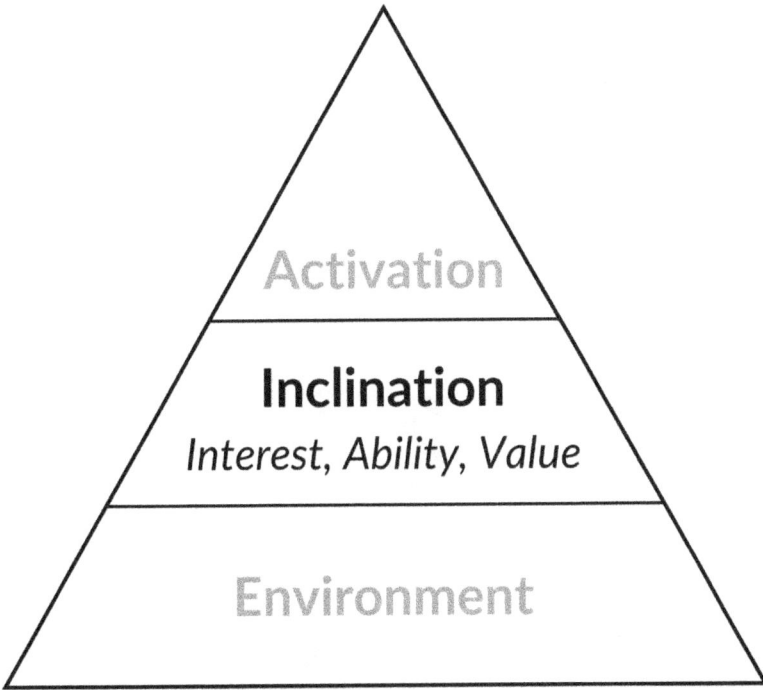

The next level of the Hierarchy of Team Engagement Needs is inclination. This level sits atop the foundation of an environment that promotes engagement and takes us from looking at external forces to internal characteristics. Three characteristics determine our inclination towards something.

1. **Interest:** the inherent curiosity or desire to explore something
2. **Ability:** the capability to carry out tasks and contribute effectively
3. **Value:** that which people consider to be important

In the following three chapters, we will explore these characteristics and how they support engagement.

Chapter 10:
Inclination—**Interest**

Interest is a psychological state of engagement.
—Annie Murphy Paul, biology and social sciences author,
magazine journalist

If interest is the psychological state of engagement, what then is disinterest?

When I was fifteen years old, I got my first job at what was then called Staples Business Depot. I was hired as a cashier. At the outset, I was grateful to have a job and excited to learn new things. Very quickly, however, the repetitive and unchallenging nature of cashier work became disengaging. I could feel myself wanting to quit, just out of boredom and a complete lack of interest—until one day when the Copy & Print Centre in the store was short staffed. With extra cashiers, the managers asked if anyone was willing to help. At the time, I was just desperate to leave the cash register, so I enthusiastically volunteered. Over in the Copy & Print Centre, customers would come in with unique projects, looking for us to help bring them to life. From birthday cards to memory albums to presentations, every day was something new! I found myself genuinely interested in these different print projects. Aware that this type of work was available, I knew I couldn't go back to the cash register. I asked my manager at the time if I could be transferred to the Copy & Print Centre. Unfortunately, he said they had enough staff and that cashiers were needed. Disappointed, I returned to the cash register for the next few shifts, where I began brainstorming an exit plan, even if that meant quitting.

If you don't solve the *interest problem* for your team, your team members will eventually solve it themselves, seeking teams and positions that align with their interests. Or worse, your team member stays with your team, grows increasingly disengaged, and weighs the team down in morale and productivity.

Luckily for me, another one of my managers *observed* how much I avoided the cash register. He noticed that I gravitated over to the Copy & Print Centre if ever they needed any help at all or if it was slow at the registers. This manager formally initiated my training in the Copy & Print Centre, and I ended up continuing to work at Staples for another five years.

When we're uninterested in tasks, we exert less discretionary effort towards those tasks. The lack of discretionary effort or disengagement could be the very reason we may appear to be unsuccessful in those areas. Gary Vee is a great example.

FROM Fs TO SUCCESS

Gary Vaynerchuk, better known as "Gary Vee," is an American businessman, author of multiple books, and a noteworthy public speaker on topics such as social media, branding, e-commerce, and more. He is the founder of VaynerMedia, Empathy Wines, and Resy and is also the chairman of VaynerX.

Needless to say, Gary Vee has built a successful career and is very well-known in the media.

However, not everyone saw this coming. Particularly Gary's school teachers. Gary Vaynerchuk was a terrible student. His report cards were full of Ds and Fs, with the occasional A in gym class. Because of this track record, Gary was told that he was going to be a failure. His teachers simply thought he was lazy and, unfortunately, they didn't see the bigger picture. They failed to recognize that Gary's interests simply were elsewhere. Instead of dedicating his time and energy to getting good grades, Gary found himself interested in business and engaged himself in growing his family's wine business. Gary Vee was responsible for growing this business from $3 million in annual revenue to $60 million. Quite the opposite of failure.

Gary explains his disinterest in school in this quote about laziness: "I think being lazy is a good thing. Because I think that if you're lazy, you're actually giving yourself an indication that you don't like it."[61]

The difference between disengagement and engagement can simply be a lack of interest.

The reason that interest is linked to engagement is because interest is the source of curiosity. When we're interested in something, we're curious about potential outcomes, which means we pay closer attention and even process information more efficiently. Interest naturally encourages us to work harder and to persist longer when the task becomes challenging. When we're disinterested in a task, hard work and persistence don't seem worth it because we're simply not curious about the outcomes and would rather engage ourselves elsewhere.

Professor of Psychology Judith Harackiewicz of the University of Wisconsin writes: "Research has found that interest is a more powerful predictor of future choices than prior achievement or demographic variables."[62] In a seven-year study, Harackiewicz and her colleagues found that a college student's interest in an introductory psychology course taken in their freshman year predicted how likely they were to enroll in additional psychology classes and to major in psychology. Interest predicted these outcomes more accurately than the students' grades in the initial course.[63]

Regardless of whether we're good at something or not, interest is the force that naturally draws our attention and energy towards a task, creating engagement. On the other hand, disinterest leads to subconscious avoidance of a task as our minds instinctively steer us away from tasks that fail to stimulate our curiosity.

Depending on where your team's interests lie, it is a powerful force that is either leading your team towards engagement at work or pulling them away from it.

DO YOU HAVE A DISINTERESTED TEAM?

I once managed a marketing team responsible for creating and designing marketing assets that included flyers, graphics, videos for social media, email newsletters, and blog posts. The team was a group of highly creative young individuals (many of them recently out of school) who had a passion for marketing and design. The work they produced was always artistic and imaginative. However, for some reason, they always missed their blog deadlines. They had received training on blog writing and were given several examples, yet their blogs consistently felt uninspired. They excelled in all their other responsibilities, but for some reason, their work always fell short of expectations when it came to writing blogs. I wanted to figure out why this was. Did they not have enough training? Was the training ineffective? Were the blog briefs unclear? Was I unclear? I knew that directly asking about their blog work wasn't likely to reveal the insight I was looking for. Instead, I had one-on-one conversations with each of them about their interests and what they enjoyed working on. Their lists of interests did not include blog writing. So, I asked a follow-up question: "Where do you think it is best to focus our energies in marketing?" They said video content and social media. By the end of the conversation, it was clear that they weren't interested in blog writing because they didn't think it was an effective marketing strategy nor an effective use of their time. The avoidance, missed deadlines, and lower quality of their blog work were all symptoms of an interest problem.

Whether it's just a couple of team members or your entire team who have lost interest, an interest problem can be difficult to deal with. First, it can be difficult to deduce the fact that the team is disinterested.

A team with disinterested team members shows the following symptoms:

- Frequent mistakes due to a lack of attention to detail
- High stress levels from some not pulling their weight, forcing others to cover for them
- Decreased productivity / avoidance of certain tasks
- Decreased communication
- Low innovation / difficulty problem-solving
- Frequent absenteeism
- Reduced quality of work
- Missed deadlines

These symptoms may not always indicate that the problem is, in fact, an interest problem; however, they should encourage you to start asking the right questions.

Pro Tips: How to Overcome the Interest Problem

The interest problem is difficult to solve because it is difficult to spark someone's interest in something that they are simply not interested in. For instance, if you don't like country music, it would be difficult for me to suddenly spark your interest in country music. Perhaps one day, you experience live music in a country bar and suddenly gain a new perspective on country music, or you might listen to that one song that has you thinking, "Maybe country music ain't so bad." Many people, however, would remain steadfast in their disinterest in country music and keep their playlists filled with the genres they are interested in.

So, instead of trying to solve the interest problem by expending effort trying to change someone's interests, I offer strategies to avoid or minimize the impact of the interest problem. You can overcome interest problems *prior* to them even surfacing, address *current* interest problems in the present, or create a plan to overcome them in the *future*. Let me explain.

Overcoming the Interest Problem

Prior	**PRE-QUALIFY THEIR INTEREST**
Current	**DISTRIBUTE TASKS ACCORDING TO INTEREST** **ALIGN INTERESTS TO ASPECTS OF CURRENT ROLE**
Future	**DESIGN FUTURE PATH THAT ALIGNS WITH INTERESTS**

Overcoming the Interest Problem **Prior** to It Becoming a Problem

Imagine you're going on a first date. There has been enough chemistry between you and your potential partner that brought you from text messages and phone calls to a first date. You finally get to have an in-person conversation to talk about your interests. On that date, you start to notice your potential partner is not interested in raising a family of their own. The problem is that you've always wanted to build a large family. Once you realize that your interests don't align on important issues like this, you have two options. Either you continue to date them, hoping their interests will change, or address the lack of alignment at the beginning to avoid future issues. The latter is what I call pre-qualifying their interests.

The pre-qualification stage for any team is critical. Some differences in interests, such as a difference in interest in sports, are acceptable. Others, such as a difference in interest in the fundamental work that your team is doing, can be disastrous.

Before assigning anyone to any team, whether it's a personal relationship (a home team) or a team at work, it is in your (and your team's) greatest benefit to first understand their interests. This gives you the strategic advantage to determine whether that person is right for the team and what roles or tasks that person is best suited for.

For example, let's say that you're a customer service manager looking to expand your team. You're seeking someone to assist with entering client orders and coordinating with the production and shipping departments. In an interview, you meet a candidate who has the skills you're looking for. They have excellent communication skills, they are organized, and they are adept at project management. When you ask about their interests, however, they share that they really enjoy working with technology and automation. The customer service role involves minimal use of technology and automation.

Given the nature and the volume of work, it becomes clear that this position would not satisfy this candidate's interest in technology. Taking these differences in interest into consideration, you forward their resume to the technology and innovation team, where the candidate is better positioned to stay engaged.

Taking the time to assess interests before it becomes a problem can prevent disengagement and misalignment down the road. Simply asking someone about their interests—assuming they're honest—can reveal what truly motivates them and what will keep them engaged in their work.

Overcoming Your **Current** Interest Problem

Let's return to our first date scenario. Let's say the first date went well, and your interests aligned. Fast forward six months and the relationship has progressed. You just started renting an apartment together. Living with one another in this new space has brought some issues to the surface that you had not previously considered. You realize that your partner has absolutely no interest in cooking and would much prefer to order takeout for every meal. They enjoy the thrill of trying new things and the speed and efficiency of shopping online. While you enjoy takeout from time to time, you're much more interested in cooking at home and experimenting with new recipes—though grocery shopping isn't exactly your favourite part. Recognizing the two different interests, you both decide to assign tasks that align with each other's interests. With an interest in trying new foods and shopping, that partner will research ingredients for fun and exciting new meals and do the grocery shopping. The partner interested in cooking will put together new recipes at home. Both partners are engaged in their tasks and feel that their team is performing to the best of its ability.

When you discover a *current* interest problem where the interests of your team don't align with their work or their role, ask yourself:

- Can I **distribute or redistribute tasks** according to interest?

- Can I **align their interests to aspects of the current role**?

I'll share examples of how you might do both.

Distribution According to Interest

The used car industry can be a tough business. It is historically known to be a low-trust environment. People often view used car sales representatives as untrustworthy and also tend to be skeptical about the quality of the cars they're selling. I was curious to know how sales representatives overcome buyer skepticism and are able to stay engaged at work. After speaking with the sales / finance manager at a used car dealership, it became apparent just how crucial interest is (no financial pun intended). He mentioned, "In car sales, engagement is everything. Customers don't want to buy from a disengaged sales representative, and so a large part of what I do is distributing customers according to interests. One rep on my team has a passion and interest in electric vehicles, so I generally assign clients seeking electric vehicles to him. However, it's not just interests related to types of cars. For example, another rep recently started a family, and his interests are now with his family. I generally assign family walk-ins to him. Matching the interests is the easiest way I create engaging conversations between my team and our clients. It keeps my team engaged, and it increases our sales."

Where possible, distributing tasks according to the different interests on your team does much of the heavy lifting in helping them stay engaged in the work that they're doing while naturally encouraging high performance.

Alignment of Interests to Current Role

Sometimes it is not feasible to distribute tasks or clients according to interest. In those instances, assess the possibility of aligning your team's interests with their current roles.

Marc Raad, the president and founder of a software automation company, Significans Automation Inc., took a unique approach to engaging his team. He recognized that one teammate in particular did not have an affinity for sales. However, being a very small team, all team members were involved in both the sales and operations of the business. In Marc's position, being unable to distribute tasks based solely on interest, he tried an alternative approach. This particular teammate had an interest in mechanics and how things work. Marc decided to give him a unique assignment. Marc instructed this team member to go to different stores that sold sewing machines. While it was a seemingly strange task, Marc emphasized that this team member should pay attention to *how* the salespeople sold the sewing machine. In particular, Marc asked him to observe the education they provide. He said, "Do they give you enough knowledge to say 'I love it. I want it. How do I get more of it?'" As someone who was already interested in the mechanical nature of the machine, this team member would naturally grasp the operational intricacies and would, therefore, have many questions for the salesperson. This team member visited multiple stores to examine different sewing machines and very quickly picked up on the different approaches and communication styles used by each salesperson. This exercise not only allowed this team member to explore his curiosity and interest, but it also led to the realization that the stores selling sewing machines best did so through education and not a high-pressure sales pitch. This made the selling process much more interesting to this teammate, who could now focus on his passion for how things work and passing that knowledge on to prospective clients.

Creating alignment between interests and responsibilities on a team, whether directly through distribution of tasks or indirectly by drawing a connection, will allow your team to feel more engaged in their work.

Overcoming Your Interest Problem in the **Future**

We're way past the first date. It has now been one year since you moved into your apartment together. The problem is that you're beginning to outgrow the space. Your partner has developed an interest in crafts. The craft supplies they've acquired are overflowing. They are crowding the small living space you have. That being said, your partner wants to buy more arts and crafts equipment. Purchasing more equipment is simply not feasible for your current space, so you cannot satisfy your partner's interest in expanding their crafting space in the present. However, this is something that can be solved in the future. You sit down to discuss the idea of moving into a larger space in the future. In order to support your partner's interests, you discuss having a dedicated crafting space in the new place and ask that your partner hold off on purchasing any new tools / equipment until then. They agree, recognizing that the current time and space do not allow for them to expand their interests. However, there is a future plan in place, which keeps them engaged in the present while remaining optimistic about the future.

In many team situations, it is difficult or impossible to make immediate changes to align your team's interests. It could be budget constraints, personnel shortages, or even a lack of opportunity. **Whatever the reason, what's not possible today may be possible tomorrow.** While you may not be able to take action immediately, creating a future plan for a team member that aligns with their interests will help support their current engagement. For example, place yourself in the role of customer service manager. Let's say that a member of your customer service team expresses an interest in moving to the sales team. The sales team is currently full. Not to mention, the customer service team is extremely busy and can't afford to lose a team member right now. As customer service manager, you know that if you don't do something to align the interests of this team member, they will become disengaged. To try and solve the interest problem, you speak to the sales manager about the future options for joining the sales team. You discover that a senior sales rep is planning to retire in one year, which will open a position on the team. You've got a plan!

Next, you have a meeting with your team member and say, *"I want to do everything I can to ensure you are engaged as part of our team. I know that sales is something that you're interested in. Currently, there are no positions open on their team. However, Charlotte is retiring next year, which will open up a spot. In the meantime, there are several skills I can help you develop here in customer service that will support your success when you transition into sales. We can even look at some of the more complex accounts we have and discuss the sales strategy behind them. The idea is that you spend the year learning and growing in customer service, and in the future, I'd be happy to support your transition into sales. How does that sound?"*

Let's unpack this detailed statement into the key components:

Demonstrate Understanding of the Team Member's Interests	*I want to do everything I can to ensure you are engaged as part of our team. I know that sales is something that you're interested in.*
Frame the Problem	*Currently, there are no positions open on their team.*
Offer the Solution	*However, Charlotte is retiring next year, which will open up a spot. In the meantime, there are several skills I can help you develop here in customer service that will support your success when you transition into sales. We can even look at some of the more complex accounts that we have and discuss the sales strategy behind them.*
Make a Commitment and Ask for Commitment	*The idea is that you spend the year learning and growing in customer service, and in the future, I'd be happy to support your transition into sales. How does that sound?*
Follow-Through	**Follow through on the commitment you made.**

The caveat to solving the interest problem in the future is the follow-through. Failing to fulfill the commitment you made will have severely damaging effects on engagement because you will have broken their trust. We know that a low-trust environment breeds doubt and disengagement. Therefore, to close the loop on the interest problem, fulfill the commitment.

Naturally, before you can solve an interest problem, you must discover what your team's interests are.

HOW TO DISCOVER YOUR TEAM'S INTERESTS

As a leader, you wear many hats, so it's practical—and often necessary—to focus on day-to-day tasks and how they align with broader organizational goals. In that context, taking the time to explore your team's individual interests may seem minor or even unnecessary. However, getting to know your team's interests will help you as a leader to make better decisions, especially those that involve your team's performance. Two ways that you can discover your team's interests are through **conversation** and **observation**.

Conversation

If you ask the right questions, people will naturally gravitate to talking about things they are interested in. As a leader, you simply take the time to engage in conversation with your team, asking open-ended questions and actively listening. Pay attention to the following:

- What do your team members enjoy talking about?
- What topics do they constantly bring up?
- What are they talking about when they seem most passionate?
- What ideas or solutions do they frequently propose?
- What personal or professional goals do they mention?
- What do they express excitement or curiosity about?
- How do they describe their successes or challenges?

Observation

Sometimes, people are not explicit about what their interests are. However, they often indicate their interests through their behaviour. You might notice them gravitating towards certain tasks or getting especially creative with certain projects. What is it about those projects or tasks that have them most engaged? If you spend time with your team and observe them doing different activities, you can find the answers to:

- What are they doing when they seem most engaged?
- What do they seem excited to do?
- What aspects of their work do they seem most invested in?
- What tasks do they avoid?
- What are they doing when they seem most disengaged?
- What types of tasks do they gravitate to?

By discovering your team's interests through conversation and observation and solving the interest problem, you build teams that are more engaged, better performing, and more likely to stay for the long term. You may be wondering, though, how you might be expected to keep track of everyone's interests and align them with their roles. I'd like to introduce a tool called the **engagement profile**.

ENGAGEMENT PROFILE

There are many objective metrics to measure performance, but generally, the metrics used to measure engagement are impersonal and lack the nuance they need. If you've ever had the experience of filling out an employee satisfaction survey, you would be familiar with Likert scale questions like:

How happy are you with your roles and responsibilities in this organization?

☐	☐	☐	☐	☐
Very Unsatisfied	Unsatisfied	Neutral	Satisfied	Very Satisfied

How satisfied are you with the overall work environment at this organization?

☐	☐	☐	☐	☐
Very Unsatisfied	Unsatisfied	Neutral	Satisfied	Very Satisfied

These surveys are generally used to provide the company with an overall employee satisfaction percentage rating and rarely provide enough information to solve the underlying problems that are impacting employee engagement. Objective measures like Likert or rating scales are used because they are quick, cheap, and easy to summarize.

If survey results say that 80% of employees are **satisfied** with the overall work environment, would this prompt change? Probably not. While 80% satisfaction may look good, it calls into question why employees aren't *"very* satisfied." Furthermore, what aspects of the environment are they satisfied / dissatisfied with and why? How is this impacting their engagement? Remember, employee satisfaction is not employee engagement, and an employee satisfaction survey cannot measure the level of discretionary effort an employee inputs. The answers you need are around *why* engagement needs are not being met, and a survey may not be able to capture the details you'd require to make impactful changes.

Inclination is all about how an individual team member relates to their role on the team. It is personal. Therefore, these generic surveys generally do not capture the data to provide the actionable insights you need as a leader. So, as a leader, I suggest adding an engagement profile to your toolkit.

An engagement profile functions similarly to a customer relationship management (CRM) tool. CRM enables you to collect and record details about customers that enrich the relationships with your customers. It could be details about the customer's preferences, past problems, current challenges, and even personal details. This information would be used to customize how you interact with the customer. For example, after recording a customer's challenges and a few personal details, you could begin your next conversation by referencing those personal touches and then offer a personalized solution to address their specific challenges. Unsurprisingly, Freshworks, a global business solution software-as-a-service (SaaS) company, conducted a survey which found that businesses that use a CRM are 86% more likely to exceed their sales goals.[64]

Similarly, an engagement profile is a tool to record this data about your team and enrich their experience in their role. It would include personalized details about each team member's interests, abilities, challenges, and values to allow you to come up with relevant ideas that support their engagement. Consider the engagement profile a living document that leaders can use to manage and organize important information about their team's inclination. Any time a new employee joins the team, you, as the leader, can initiate an engagement profile and continuously update it as the working relationship develops and you learn more about their inclination.

This is an example of what an engagement profile might look like:

Engagement Profile

Team Member: Amina
Current Role: Data Analyst

Main Responsibilities:
- Analyzing data sets to identify trends and insights
- Creating reports and dashboards for stakeholders
- Collaborating with departments to support data-driven decisions

Interests
- Storytelling with data
- Sustainability and social impact
- Mentoring
- Continuous learning and online courses

Interest-Based Engagement Ideas
- Invite her to present insights at team meetings to showcase data storytelling skills.
- Assign projects with social impact (e.g., analyzing sustainability metrics or nonprofit campaign data).
- Pair her with junior team members as a mentor or peer coach.
- Provide access to advanced analytics courses or certifications in areas of interest.
- Explore projects, partnerships, or pro bono work with mission-driven organizations to connect her values with her day-to-day work.

Ability (Skill + Capacity)

Skills
- Advanced data analysis
- Data visualization

- Statistical modeling
- Communication skills

Capacity Notes
- Amina has a significant workload
- Amina has high emotional intelligence (EQ)

Challenges (Opportunities for Growth)
- Leadership development
- Cross-functional collaboration
- Exploring advanced technologies
- Improving stakeholder engagement: Building stronger relationships with stakeholders will allow her to better understand business needs and better communicate the value of data insights.

Values
- Collaboration
- Continuous improvement
- Social impact
- Generational values (Millennial): purpose and flexibility

Using the Engagement Profile

Collecting and using this data in an engagement profile eliminates the guesswork in finding personalized strategies that effectively keep your people engaged. Over time, as you learn more about your team members, you will continue to update their engagement profiles. When it's time to launch new engagement initiatives or make decisions that impact your employees, these engagement profiles act as a valuable reference to streamline the decision-making process and increase the success rate of the initiatives. They will provide insight into what initiatives, actions, or decisions would be best received and most impactful for your team. For example, if the engagement profiles reveal that your employees are interested in continuous improvement opportunities, you might prioritize tuition reimbursement over wellness spending when deciding how to allocate resources. Not only will it yield a higher return on investment—enhancing skills that directly contribute to individual growth and organizational performance—it will also be better received by employees. It will do more to engage them than other initiatives that do not align with their interests.

Some best practices to keep in mind when adopting engagement profiles include:

- Don't turn the completion of an engagement profile into a formal interview. It will feel like a disingenuous corporate box-checking exercise to your employees. Instead, this information should be collected through a combination of casual conversations, observations, and informal check-in meetings.
- Check-in meetings should be genuine, informal meetings for open communication that allow team members to share updates, concerns, and feedback (not just about work).
- Engagement profiles are a leadership tool and should not necessarily be shared with team members. In the same way that you would not share the CRM profile with a customer and instead simply use it to guide interactions, communication, and decisions, the engagement profile is not meant to be shared with the team members.

In the following chapter, we explore how an employee's ability supports inclination to their role and their engagement.

Chapter 11:
Inclination—**Ability**

Your workforce is your most valuable asset. The knowledge and skills they have represent the fuel that drives the engine of business—and you can leverage that knowledge.
—Harvey Mackay, businessman and author

At the time of this writing (as of August 2024), Apple Inc. was the largest company in the world by market capitalization.[65] What's interesting about Apple is the consistent brand experience in their stores. Whenever you walk into an Apple store, you know exactly what to expect: a sleek, minimalist store design, with interactive product displays and friendly staff ready to help. Apple's store employees, whom they call "Geniuses," are known for their insightful advice and accurate representation of the company's brand.[66] How does a company so large reach such service excellence with their team members so consistently?

APPLE STARTS WITH ABILITY

Referring back to the Hierarchy of Team Engagement Needs, ability is the second characteristic of the inclination level. To support the inclination towards a particular project or goal, a team member must have the **ability** to carry out their tasks. Without ability, the team member may struggle to meet expectations and to contribute effectively. When team members feel incapable, it leads to their frustration and decreased motivation, ultimately hindering the overall progress of the project or goal.

As you would expect, a high-performing team has an inherent focus on building the ability of the team. **Without ability, there is no performance.** It seems fundamental, however, in order to maximize ability, we must look at the two considerations that impact it: skill and capacity.

Ability = Skill + Capacity

- **Skill**: refers to the training or knowledge required to perform the task.
- **Capacity**: refers to the potential or maximum amount that someone can produce or perform. Capacity includes one's physical capacity, mental / cognitive capacity, and personal capacity.

To maximize the ability of their team members, Apple combines a strong training and development program to enhance employees' skills with a highly selective recruitment process that seeks those with high capacity.

Apple "Geniuses" are required to know extensive amounts of technical information and be able to simplify it for a less technical audience. When you consider how frequently Apple launches new products and updates, a way to keep the team informed at all times is a necessity. Their training program is a multi-faceted, multi-pathway program that includes e-learning, on-the-job learning, and peer-to-peer learning. Apple also supports their team through continuous learning programs and the "Hello" app. This is an internal app which shares daily briefings and important company news with employees.[67]

Apple's training program ensures team members are well-supported with the skills they need to work effectively. However, before new team members even begin this training process, Apple has assessed their capacity during the selection process. With such a high demand for technical knowledge, Apple seeks candidates with a high technological capacity. This means that candidates have some background or affinity towards technology, indicating that they have the capacity to understand the technical nature of Apple's products and to continuously build on that knowledge.[68]

The dual focus on skill and capacity has produced a high level of performance ability and a 90% employee retention rate for the company. To put this in perspective, the average employee turnover rate for retail is around 60%, which means that over half of the employees in the organization will leave within the year.[69] Meanwhile, 90% of Apple's employees will stay. That's impressive.

DELOITTE AND PERFORMANCE EXCELLENCE

Have you ever had the experience of having to pick up the slack for a low-performing team member? Did the surprising lack of ability and the extra strain it placed on your team have you wondering what went wrong in the hiring and selection process?

This is not the case at Deloitte.

Deloitte is a global business services organization specializing in providing audit and assurance, consulting, financial advisory, risk advisory, tax, and related services.[70] Having served approximately 90% of Fortune 500 companies,

Deloitte has a reputation for high performance. According to a Gartner June 2023 report, Deloitte had been ranked #1 by revenue for the sixth year in a row and the eleventh time overall. The company also received the best possible rating in Gartner's 2023 Vendor Rating report, ranking first in business and technology consulting services for the second consecutive year.[71]

With over 450,000 employees globally, I wondered what their secret to achieving such high engagement and high levels of performance was. After interviewing a former Deloitte employee, the connection between their commitment to service excellence and their investment in *ability* became clear.

With Deloitte's reputation, it's no secret that having Deloitte on your resume is an asset. That being said, Deloitte receives thousands upon thousands of applications in a year. In order to maintain their reputation, they rigorously screen for high-capacity talent. This includes a robust rating system that rates candidates on important competencies such as the capacity for leadership, critical thinking, and self-reliance in addition to any inclination for any technical skills required for the position. The recruitment process is highly selective, seeking those with the highest possible capacity for their most valued qualifications. This process takes time and the collaborative effort of multiple team members who analyze candidates.

To maximize *ability*, once high-capacity candidates have been selected, they experience an intensive training program through "Deloitte University," or "DU." This consists of highly interactive, experiential leader-led programs designed to inspire and accelerate development.[72] These programs are targeted towards specific promotions. For instance, going from consultant to senior consultant requires completion of the Senior Consultant Program in "DU."

According to the former Deloitte consultant, the training programs are highly sought after by team members for their exceptional value. They include simulated client engagements and business case studies that reflect the clients' challenges. Team members collaborate to present solutions tailored to both the business and the client's profile. The training even includes teaching participants to recognize and work effectively with different personality types. The program also incorporates modules on storytelling techniques and empathy building, offering a well-rounded and impactful learning experience with proven results in producing high-performing team members.

Deloitte's approach is to focus on inclination and double down on ability. What Deloitte has done is be selective with their candidates to ensure they have the **capacity** to succeed in their role and then vigorously build their **skills**. This approach has been immensely successful in contributing to both Deloitte's performance and profitability.

Let's explore skill and capacity further.

SKILL

Skill refers to the training or knowledge required to perform a task.

For example, based on the requirements of their role, does your team know how to:

- use the company software?
- analyze sales data?
- complete customer reports?
- operate equipment?
- deliver a sales pitch?

Having the right skills determines whether someone can complete the job. If a team member does not have the skills they need, training can fill the knowledge / skills gap. A large part of performance depends on how well employees are trained in the skills that they need. The better trained they are, the more likely they are to deliver the desired outcome.

After all, how would a team that doesn't know how to:

- use the company software *keep projects organized?*
- analyze sales data *make decisions to improve sales?*
- complete customer reports *give customers the information they need?*
- operate equipment *manufacture the product your organization sells?*
- deliver a sales pitch *grow the business and win new clients?*

Ensuring your team has the skill set is just half the battle in ensuring your team has the ability for high performance.

Why Skill Without Capacity Is Not Enough

Skill is knowing HOW to do something, and capacity is HOW WELL someone is able to do it.

Building your team's skills without considering their capacity will not lead to sustainable performance. For example, imagine that you are a basketball coach and have a player who is skilled in shooting a basketball. They know how to play the game, and they know how to shoot; however, their fitness level is poor. They have difficulty keeping up on the court and cannot operate at the same level as other players simply because their physical capacity has not been increased. Their ability for high performance in basketball depends not only on skill but also on capacity.

Another example is sales. Your sales team may know HOW to deliver a sales presentation. They might know all the features and benefits of your products and services. However, if they do not have the capacity for understanding and listening to the customer's unique situation, they will be far less effective at closing deals. A team member who has developed the capacity for listening, understanding, and doing what is best for the potential client will perform better. Because it's not just about knowing HOW to do something; it's also about increasing your capacity to do it better.

Sometimes, capacity is not just a function of one's own internal limitations, but may also encompass the external limitations placed upon them. You may have a highly skilled employee whose capacity is limited by the resources available to them, the volume of demand placed on them, or any external obstacles that prevent them from performing at their best.

For example, in the same sales role, perhaps a team member has been given an extremely high workload, with no resources to support them. As a result, that team member cannot deliver high-quality service to customers simply because their limited time and effort is spread between far too many tasks. In this case, the organization can increase that team member's capacity by either reducing the workload or providing resources such as software tools or automation functions that increase their capacity to manage more tasks.

External limitations might also include challenging personal circumstances. You may have an employee with a sick relative who now has caretaker responsibilities. They need to manage appointments, medications, daily routines, and provide emotional support—all while trying to maintain their performance at work. Their capacity is limited due to the emotional stress of being a caretaker and the pressure and responsibility that comes with it.

That being said, as a leader, understanding capacity is helpful in helping you take action. Being aware of both **internal capacity** and **external capacity** will allow you to make the adjustments, accommodations, and improvements that will increase the collective *ability* of your team.

Internal Capacity

- **Physical Capacity**: Do they have the physical attributes to perform the task? Are they in proper physical condition to meet the expectations?
- **Mental / Emotional Capacity**: Do they have the cognitive capacity for problem-solving and critical thinking? Do they have emotional capacity such as empathy and self-awareness? Do they have mental / emotional capacity based on other stressors in their life (grief, loss, pain)?

External Capacity

- **Demand Capacity**: Are there too many demands placed on the team member, forcing them to reduce the time and attention spent on each demand? Is your team weighed down by tedious, repetitive tasks or problems?
- **System / Resource Capacity**: Can the organizational systems in place support the team effectively? Do team members get answers efficiently? Do things operate efficiently? Are there enough resources to support the performance of your team? Does your team have what they need to complete tasks efficiently?

Expanding capacity means creating the space—whether through time, resources, or support—for employees to fully apply their skills and face challenges without becoming overburdened. However, it is all about balance.

ABILITY AND CHALLENGE, A FINELY BALANCED RELATIONSHIP

The relationship between the *ability* of a team member and the *challenge* of their role is one to pay attention to. Matching challenge with ability is a determining factor in one's inclination towards a task and is, therefore, connected to engagement.

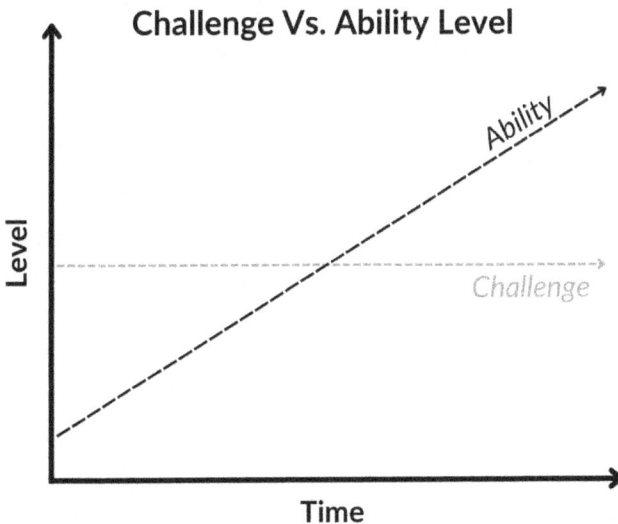

Challenge Vs. Ability Level

Level (y-axis), Time (x-axis), Ability (rising dashed line), Challenge (horizontal dashed line)

If we look at the challenge vs. ability level chart, we'll see that one's ability can change over time. This is a result of training, development, and experience. The level of challenge is fixed in the role until the responsibilities or circumstances change.

When the Challenge Is Too High

Imagine going to the gym with your personal trainer for the first time. As you start your training journey, your trainer expects you to bench press 400 pounds. If you were not already a bodybuilder, you would look at your personal trainer as if they were crazy. You wouldn't be inclined to attempt a lift that you know is impossible, given your current ability level.

When the ability level is far below the challenge level, meaning that the challenge is too great for the team member, they will feel disinclined due to feelings of overwhelm and inadequacy. In their mind, they feel that they are faced with an impossible task and wonder why they should even bother trying.

When the Challenge Is Too Low

On the opposite end of the spectrum, if the ability level is far above the challenge level, meaning the challenge is far too easy for the team member, they will feel bored. An extremely easy task will feel like a waste of their time and ability. If your personal trainer asked you to bench press five pounds (again, assuming you are far stronger than that), you would wonder why you're even paying this trainer.

You would not feel inclined to perform a task that is so far below your ability level because your skills and capacity are being underutilized. Tasks that lack challenge lack any sense of accomplishment and lead to disengagement.

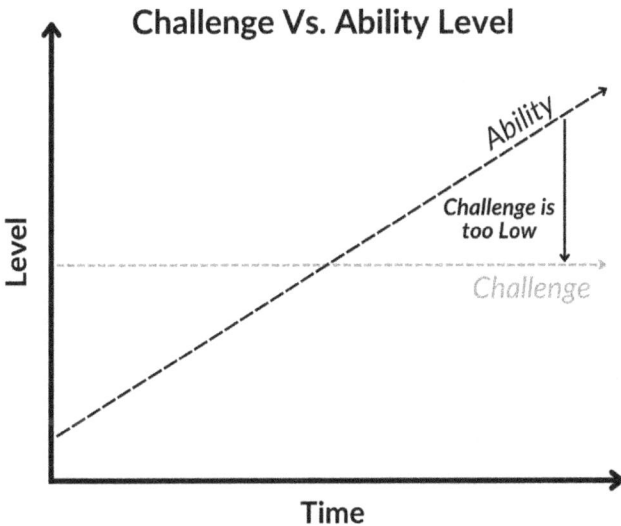

Challenge Vs. Ability Level

Ability

Challenge is too Low

Challenge

Level

Time

The Inclination Zone, When Challenge Is Just Right

When it comes to inclination and ability, team members require adequate challenge. The challenge level needs to match the ability level more closely. In other words, your personal trainer should give you exercises that match your ability but also challenge you enough so that you improve over time. The goal is to find weight that is difficult enough but not impossible.

I call this the **inclination zone**: the area near the crossover point between ability and challenge.

Challenge Vs. Ability Level

The inclination zone is where the challenge level just slightly exceeds the ability level, presenting the team with a challenge that encourages them to push past their current limits. That hustle turns into a sense of gratification and accomplishment once they've increased their ability level to meet that level of challenge.

This would be similar to the process of trying to increase your maximum bench press weight by twenty pounds. The challenge is doable, so you're engaged in the process, and you push yourself to add a few pounds every week. When the day finally comes when you've increased your ability—you've increased your maximum weight by twenty pounds, you feel a sense of accomplishment for your efforts.

As a leader, there will likely be times when you are expected to deliver results that seem far out of reach for your team. What do you do if the challenge you've been given considerably exceeds the ability of your team?

Using the Inclination Zone When Challenge Exceeds Ability

Thursday, June 13, 2019, in Toronto, was a day like no other. I remember the chanting in the streets of the city, with thousands of people wearing red and black celebrating with one another. The streets were crowded like I had never seen. People were jumping and cheering in the middle of intersections, completely ignoring the traffic. The city was alive all night as we stayed up late, celebrating. I had never seen Toronto so happy.

In my lifetime, growing up in Toronto (and the Greater Toronto Area), there had never been a significant sports event. Our sports teams were relatively ordinary and had never won a championship. But that changed on June 13, 2019, when the Toronto Raptors defeated the Golden State Warriors in the NBA Finals.

Prior to 2019, the Raptors had never won an NBA Championship in their history. So, if we had to map the Raptors ability versus the challenge of winning the NBA Championship, it might have looked like this:

Challenge Vs. Ability Level

Inclination Zone

Ability

Level

Pre 2019 Toronto Raptors

Challenge (Winning the NBA Championship)

Time

In 2018, however, leadership changed. Nick Nurse was hired as the new head coach. What should a leader do when faced with a situation where the challenge exceeds the team's ability? When the team is far from the inclination zone?

Nick Nurse employed many of the engagement strategies discussed in this book, including building positive team culture and fostering trust in the team environment. When it comes to winning sports championships, however, *ability* plays a significant role.

In an interview with JJ Redick, Nick Nurse was asked, "What makes a good coach?" To answer this question, Nick Nurse shared his coaching philosophy. He said, "First, you must instill that you're playing to win the game."[73] By doing this, Nurse set the **challenge** level for the team.

Nurse goes on to say, "Can we increase each player's value in the marketplace?"[74] This means increasing their statistics to achieve better contracts, to achieve better starting positions, and to get better opportunities. Nurse explains that in order to do this, he spends a lot of time trying to get each player better and develop their **ability**. For example, he might first begin with the challenge of improving shooting accuracy by taking time to focus on "tinkering" with a player's shot.

Nick Nurse also recognizes that different players require different development. For instance, rookies require one year just to figure out how to play defence in the NBA league. This attention to increasing the ability of each individual team member to rise to the challenge was instrumental in Nick Nurse leading the Raptors to success.

By focusing on one smaller challenge at a time, Nick Nurse brings the player back into the inclination zone. When Nurse first arrived as head coach, improving shooting accuracy or learning defensive strategies would have seemed much more attainable than winning the NBA championship. By breaking the larger goal into smaller, progressive challenges, he steadily built the team's skills, capacity, and engagement—ultimately positioning them to meet the bigger objective.

Challenge Vs. Ability Level

Level

Time

Ability

Pre 2019
Toronto
Raptors

New
Inclination
Zone

Challenge
(Winning the
NBA
Championship)

Challenge
(Improve Shooting
Accuracy)

Pro Tip: Simple Steps to Increasing Ability

Enhancing team performance by increasing ability requires a focus on the following steps:

1. Map your team's current ability level, taking note of their skills and capacity. (You might record this in the *engagement profile.*)
2. Focus on a challenge within the inclination zone. (Follow the Goldilocks Rule: not too hard, not too easy.)
3. Develop your team's ability to rise to the challenge.
   a. Provide training to improve their skills.
   b. Maximize their capacity with tools, resources, and support.
4. Celebrate their increased ability, then focus on the next level of challenge.

At this point, you've solved the *interest* problem and have elevated your team's *ability.* To be fully inclined, we must also look at value.

Chapter 12:
Inclination—**Value**

People will always have options, but it's up to you to discover what they value to make sure you're the first choice.
— Ashley Chappelle, entrepreneur

In 2018, as a Millennial, I realized just how much I valued purpose and flexibility. At the time, I was working for a company that was over sixty years old. Its structure aligned very well with the values of Baby Boomers and Gen Xers. The company offered great salaries, great benefits, stability, and independence. Despite this, they had a Millennial retention problem. With an aging workforce, continuity planning and succession were a priority. The plan was to train the next generation to take over, but Millennial turnover was high. Leaders wondered why there was difficulty attracting and retaining Millennial talent. Although they offered many benefits, the truth was that the work was monotonous and the hours were strict. At the time, there was no option for hybrid or remote work. Unbeknownst to the company's leadership, this lack of flexibility and monotony was suffocating to a Millennial. The stark misalignment of values led to their disinclination, their disengagement, and ultimately their resignation. The point is, before you start thinking that *this new generation is just not built the same*, understand the differences between generational values. Assess whether your organization or team aligns with the values of the people you're trying to attract and retain. After all, it is easier to change your processes to accommodate generational values than it is to change the values of the generation.

In an article published in *Forbes*, Jason Richmond talks about employee retention strategies for Gen Z and Millennials. In the workplace, Gen Z has come to be known as the "restless generation," highly prone to job hopping or leaving their jobs even without having another one to move on to if they feel disengaged. Among strategies such as dynamic onboarding processes, training, and upward mobility, Jason mentions flexibility and adjustable working hours as common expectations of these generations.[75] The bottom line is that generational values are worth paying attention to. The engagement strategies that work with some generations won't work with others. If you fail to pay attention, you'll be paying the costs of disengagement and high turnover.

GENERATIONAL VALUES

If you've ever heard someone say, "This new generation is just *not built the same*," then you're familiar with the fact that there are differences in generational values. **Values** are simply the things that people consider to be important. In a professional sense, we are focusing on the things that people consider to be important *about their work*. The universal truth is that what may matter to one generation does not necessarily matter to another. Generational values are shaped by the collective experiences of a group of people. Those experiences are influenced by the social climate, technology, and environment at the time of their development.

- **Baby Boomers (born 1946–1964) Value Stability and Benefits**: To Baby Boomers, hard work is very important. They are known for high levels of commitment and loyalty, which were rewarded with promotions and career advancements. From their employers, Baby Boomers expect and value stability and benefits such as retirement / pension plans or health care benefits.[76]

- **Gen X (born 1965–1980) Value Independence and Balance**: Growing up, Gen X watched their Baby Boomer parents working extremely hard, leading them to seek more work-life balance. Gen X values their independence, preferring to work on teams that allow for autonomy and have minimal supervision. Gen X prefers to be self-sufficient and seeks to develop skills that support this self-sufficiency.[77]

- **Millennials (born 1981–1996) Value Purpose and Flexibility**: From a young age, Millennials were encouraged to follow their dreams and to choose meaningful work that would allow them to make an impact on society. Speaking from experience, we wanted jobs that gave us purpose. Millennials value impact and corporate social responsibility. Because of the emphasis on meaningful work, Millennials easily become disengaged when their work feels monotonous and repetitive. For this reason, Millennials value flexibility—hybrid / remote work options or flexible hours that allow them to change up their workday or work environment.

- **Generation Z (born 1997–2010) Value Technology and Inclusion**: Gen Z is characterized by their early experiences with technology and their upbringing in an internet-connected society. As a result, Gen Z tends to be highly collaborative, using a variety of digital tools to stay connected and work together.[78] Gen Z prefers to stay up to date on the latest trends and expects to work in places that use up-to-date technology. Technology inherently enables flexibility, so flexibility is something that Gen Z expects. Gen Z is also highly socially aware. They are engaged in current social issues and value diversity, equity, and inclusion. Highly tech-savvy, Gen Z is remarkably self-reliant when it comes to learning and experimenting. They often turn to platforms like YouTube and social media to find tutorials and solutions. This encourages their creative freedom as they often explore entrepreneurship or "side hustles."

- **Generation Alpha (2010–2024) Value Technology and Personalization**: Gen Alpha is an entirely digital generation. Technology is highly integrated into their daily routines, and they are familiar with the power of artificial intelligence. AI's integration into education and toys is fostering emotional intelligence, personalized learning, and rapid growth among these individuals.[79] With high technological and AI integration from a young age, Gen Alpha expects their experiences to be highly personalized.

These differences in generational values influence what each generation expects and how each generation behaves on teams. Values, particularly the alignment of work and values, are the third characteristic of a team's inclination. **When our work does not align with our values, we find it more difficult to be engaged.** When values are not aligned, we find ourselves in a state of cognitive dissonance. Cognitive dissonance is the mental discomfort that results from holding conflicting beliefs or values.[80] In our subconscious effort to resolve our cognitive dissonance, the misalignment of values can cause disinclination towards our work and eventually our disengagement.

MISALIGNMENT OF VALUES ⟶ DISINCLINATION ⟶ DISENGAGEMENT

With regard to *generational values*, the key for leaders is to be aware of the generations that make up the team and ensure the organization's practices—

and even specific roles—align with the values and expectations of each group. To ensure inclination and the alignment of values on your team, you might ask:

- **For Baby Boomers,** does your team offer stability?
- **For Gen X**, does your team offer independence and work-life balance?
- **For Millennials**, does your team provide purpose and flexibility?
- **For Gen Z**, does your team utilize technology, offer avenues for creativity, and prioritize inclusion?
- **For Gen Alpha** (although not currently old enough for the workforce), does your team offer high technological integration and personalized experiences?

Without these values, sustaining inclination is impossible. As a Millennial myself, I've experienced the exact process of disinclination due to a misalignment of values.

Generational values, however, are just one way to categorize the values of your team. In addition to considering generational values, it is helpful to consider what *type of thinking* your team members value.

LEFT-BRAIN, RIGHT-BRAIN DOMINANCE THEORY

You may have heard people describe themselves as more of a right-brain or left-brain dominant thinker. According to left-brain, right-brain dominance theory, people who are left-brain dominant thinkers are described as being logical and analytical. They are said to prefer tasks that require logical reasoning, linear problem-solving, and structured thinking. According to the theory, jobs in accounting, engineering, law, information technology, and data analysis appeal to them. Right-brain dominant thinkers are considered intuitive, creative, and subjective. They are said to prefer tasks that allow for artistic expression, creative problem-solving, big-picture thinking, and connection. According to the theory, jobs in marketing, the arts, architecture, counselling, and communications appeal to them.

LEFT-BRAIN

- Logical
- Analytical
- Practical
- Objective
- Methodical
- Structured

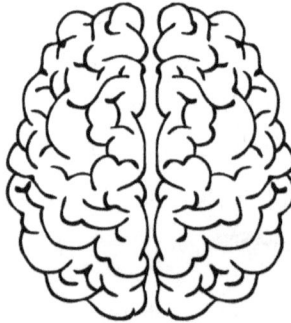

RIGHT-BRAIN

- Creative
- Emotional
- Intuitive
- Subjective
- Expressive
- Spontaneous

Brain Image Credit: "GDJ" from Pixabay

It turns out this theory is a myth. Neuroscientists have confirmed that both sides of the brain collaborate to perform tasks. Scientifically, there is no evidence to prove that people use one side of their brain more than the other.[81]

Although this is more fiction than it is fact, the left-brain, right-brain dominance theory provides an important lesson in values. The general preference of what's classified as left-brain or right-brain thinking indicates what a person values when it comes to team performance. A team of left-brain thinkers will want to see statistics and numbers, while a team of right-brain thinkers will value the opportunity to be creative, look at the bigger picture, and use their intuition to make decisions. Both groups simply consider different things to be important when making decisions and choosing how to approach tasks.

In truth, a high-performing team requires both left-brain and right-brain thinkers. The balance between logical reasoning and big-picture creative thinking contributes to success. This is why successful organizations will have a marketing department and an accounting department. The right-brainers come up with big ideas to grow, while the left-brainers assess what is feasible and how to execute these ideas.

Although both right-brainers and left-brainers are equally important, you cannot engage them in the same way. A left-brain thinker would be frustrated if all team decisions were made intuitively, while a right-brain thinker would be disengaged by constant quantitative analysis to come to a decision. When trying to build a more engaged team, it is important to identify what the members of your team value and speak to those values. The next time you call a team meeting to share information, engage the left-brainers with the logical reasoning behind the information and engage the right-brainers with the big picture and interpersonal impact of the information.

But let's not forget that everyone has a unique experience and, therefore, everyone has unique *personal* values. Although categorizing people into generations and left-brain vs. right-brain thinkers is helpful, those are still generalizations. Someone may be part of the Gen X cohort with left-brain tendencies, however, there are other personal values at play that could help leaders build a more engaged team.

PERSONAL VALUES

Growing up, my parents made it a priority for us to have dinner together as a family and talk about the events of the day. We weren't allowed to have TVs or devices in our rooms. My parents valued quality time and communication, feeling that devices in personal spaces reduced opportunities for family connection. These values of connection and uninterrupted communication became important values of mine, even at work. To my surprise, not everyone grew up this way. One evening (as a teenager in the early 2010s), I was invited to have dinner at a friend's house. I found it strange to watch everyone come to the kitchen to dish out their plates and then return to their rooms to eat instead of eating together at the table. I was shocked to discover that each family member had their own TV and their own computer in their room. My friend told me that each family member had different interests, so they wanted to be able to watch the programs they liked and have the tools to pursue those individual interests. In contrast to my own, their family valued independence, privacy, and personal pursuits.

The values we hold are often rooted in those imparted to us by our families, which differ greatly from household to household. While one family might emphasize discipline and independence, another may prioritize values such as creative expression, cultural heritage, or even emotional intelligence. These foundational values are then shaped and sometimes reshaped by the social environments we grow up in.

Outside of the family, our surroundings—friends, schools, neighbourhoods, and communities—also play a significant role in influencing what we come to value. For example, growing up in a community marked by constant change, unpredictability, or hardship can lead us to develop an appreciation for stability, security, and consistency.

Beyond this, each individual also undergoes unique life experiences—successes, failures, relationships, and challenges—that further refine their personal value system. **As a result, our personal values are developed from a complex blend of upbringing, social surroundings, and personal encounters and continue to evolve through new experiences.** All of this demonstrates that individuals, regardless of generational differences or supposed right- vs. left-brain dominance, may bring unique personal values to your team. As a leader, it helps to discover what they are and how they align with your team. It could be as simple as including a question in an interview, such as: What are three things you value most in an organization or team? Or it may call for more formal data collection methods, especially when working with large teams.

Gathering Personal Value Data for Large Teams

Leaders of very large teams may find it difficult to tap into the personal values of each of their team members. This may be too large a task. In this specific case, a survey might prove to be an effective tool. Particularly useful for a large group would be ranking questions where participants can sort their values in order of what is most important to them. For example:

Please rank the following values from **1 (most important)** to **10 (least important)** based on what matters most to you in your work environment and experience.

Rank	Value
	Job Security
	Compensation and Benefits
	Work-Life Balance
	Independence
	Purpose
	Flexibility
	Collaboration
	Technology and Innovation
	Career Growth
	Rewards and Recognition

Although personalized, qualitative information about employee values will give you a better understanding of what truly matters to your employees, sometimes generalized data is more practical to work with. This is similar to how governments are tasked with making decisions that reflect a collective summary of the population's values. The important part is that you are taking action to gain an understanding of the values of your team and making an effort to align their work with their values. An alignment of values contributes to their inclination and, ultimately, their engagement.

ALIGNMENT OF VALUES $\longrightarrow$ **INCLINATION** $\longrightarrow$ **ENGAGEMENT**

AFFECTIVE COMMITMENT

Ashley Chappelle, the founder of a Toronto-based event staffing agency, introduced me to the concept of affective commitment. The event staffing business comes with many challenges, primarily keeping staff committed and engaged. This industry has very high turnover and attracts people who enjoy the "gig economy" and social events. When I asked Ashley how she keeps her staff engaged in an industry with such high turnover and low commitment, she explained how she employs **affective commitment**.

According to *The Oxford Review*, affective commitment refers to an employee's emotional attachment and identification with an organization.[82] It is characterized by a strong sense of belonging, loyalty, and dedication towards the organization. Employees with high levels of affective commitment are deeply engaged with their work, exhibit enthusiasm, and are more likely to remain with the organization even amidst challenges.[83] Affective commitment shares many characteristics with employee engagement, though it leans more to the emotional connection, enthusiasm, and excitement towards the work and the organization.

In an interview with Ashley, when I asked how she is able to achieve affective commitment in a low-commitment and high-turnover industry, she explained that she focuses on values. "First, I have an understanding of the values of the age group / generation and the type of people that I am dealing with. I do a lot of research to identify relevant topics for them and find ways to incorporate those things. This also helps me adjust how I approach them. For example, my staff are generally not people who like to read long emails or texts, but they will be quick to respond to a voice note. More importantly, I've learned that my staff value exclusive perks, rewards, and opportunities. So, I put a lot of work into seeking out unique invitations, experiences, or opportunities to reward their commitment. I am constantly networking and building my personal brand to help me access these opportunities. My staff benefit from the connections and perks that come from all this outreach and business development. You can see the excitement in our group chats. They are constantly active, demonstrating the team's enthusiasm and eagerness to seize the opportunities. The staff also value social connection and enjoying the work that they do. I invest significant effort into booking staff with complementary personalities to create synergies at events and so that they enjoy working with one another. We value the great work we do together and the rewards that come with it."

In many high-turnover industries like staffing and even retail, little attention is paid to employment engagement. Leaders have grown to expect high turnover in these industries and, therefore, often think of employee engagement as a poor investment. In some cases, especially in the staffing industry, leaders often neglect employee engagement because they simply expect that employees *should be* engaged because employees are getting "a good opportunity." This perspective is deeply flawed and fails to draw the connection between engagement, reduced turnover, and increased profitability. The fact of the matter is that employees have options. If something better presents itself, the question is: **What is stopping them from leaving your organization?** As a way to maintain engagement in a low-commitment and high-turnover industry, Ashley Chappelle focused on aligning organizational operations with her team's values. As a result, she created a sense of affective commitment and engagement at a company that attracts and maintains talent. For her, this has led to an increase in performance, profitability, and business growth.

Value is the final characteristic of inclination for engaged teams. When our **values, interests,** and **abilities** are aligned, all the needs for a person's internal inclination to the team and to their role are satisfied. When inclination is satisfied, it translates into positive engagement economics.

Inclination Key Takeaways: Compromise Is Not Always Best

In the Hierarchy of Team Engagement Needs, the second tier, inclination, is something that is very personal. It describes the characteristics that make us feel aligned with and well-suited for our work. This tier is critical for engagement because, yes, we may have the right environment to support performance, but is the individual a fit for the role and for the team? Are they *interested*, are they *able,* and do their *values* align?

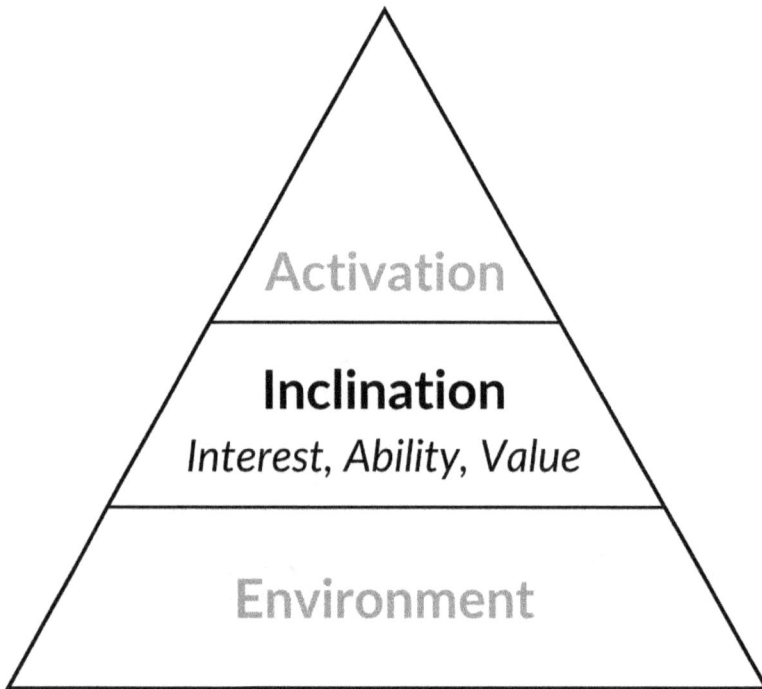

We underestimate just how important inclination is. We can run, but we cannot hide from our team's inclination needs. The problem is that many leaders are put into positions where they require their team to *compromise* on areas of their inclination. This often looks like having the team do tasks / jobs that do not match their interests, abilities, or values. It is usually out of necessity—the need to fill a role or a gap in operations. While there are parts of every job that are less "sexy" than others (we all have those annoying tasks that just have to be done), I am referring to the main tasks that make up the core responsibilities of each role. When team members are asked to compromise on their interests, abilities, or values in the main responsibilities of their roles, over time, it will sacrifice their engagement. Without meeting inclination needs, engagement cannot be supported.

I once saw stark mistakes in inclination by a leader in a change management consulting / training firm. This leader was hired in a business development capacity to both grow the business and increase the profitability of the organization. The organization already had a strong environmental foundation, with high trust, positive culture, room for expansion, and a sense of control. There was one hire, in particular (we'll call her Adina), who was extremely passionate about the learning and development industry and came with a wealth of skills and experience. She was skilled in training needs analysis, program design, content development, and learning delivery. Having been hired into a learning and development role at the change management organization, she expected to leverage the full breadth of her expertise and contribute across the diverse functions within the field. However, the leader felt task specialization was a better business approach. Task specialization involves dividing tasks into smaller, more focused roles in order to increase efficiency and expertise. As a result of the task specialization approach, this leader separated the learning and development function into three roles: training needs analysis, training design, and training delivery / facilitation. Despite her interests and abilities in all three areas, Adina was pigeonholed into working only on training design.

Adina also valued continuous improvement and variety in her role. However, this leader was of the opinion that time spent by employees attending professional development opportunities was lost production hours for the organization. He denied professional development opportunities and declined requests for an increase in variety. Although she compromised at first, Adina began to feel less and less inclined for the role. She felt her abilities exceeded the level of challenge, her interests were not being satisfied, and her values for continuous learning and flexibility were not being met. That disinclination led to disengagement until she ultimately sought employment at a different organization. The lesson? Counter to the leader's intentions to increase profitability, compromising inclination cost the business in:

- discretionary effort as Adina grew less engaged with her work.
- recruitment and onboarding costs to replace her.

- lost opportunity costs from tapping into the rest of her expertise and experience.

An investment in solving the interest problem, increasing your team's ability by building their skills to meet new levels of challenge, and aligning their roles as best as possible to their values, pays off. The better these characteristics of inclination match, the better performance, more engagement, and greater profitability you'll see from your team.

For inclination, we must be *interested*, we must be *able*, and we must be aligned with our *values*. Once these characteristics are satisfied, it lays the foundation for the next level of engagement: activation.

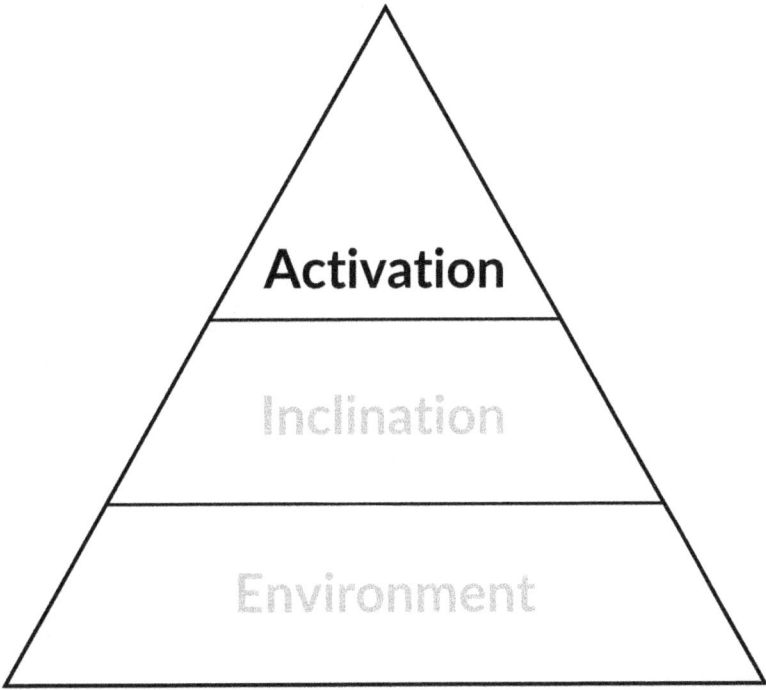

Chapter 13: Activation

If you want to change the world, start off by making your bed.
—Admiral McRaven, United States Navy

In 2014, Admiral William McRaven of the United States Navy delivered a commencement speech to the graduating class of the University of Texas. The speech is famously known as the "Make Your Bed" speech. In this speech, Admiral McRaven shares ten lessons about changing the world that he learned during the six-month Navy SEALs training.

Every morning during training, the instructors would inspect the beds of the recruits to ensure they were made to perfection. The corners would be square, the covers would be pulled tight, the pillow would be centred, and the extra blanket folded neatly at the foot of the rack—a seemingly unimportant task, considering the responsibilities of a Navy SEAL—however, there was an important lesson. That lesson was that if you make your bed every morning, you will have accomplished the first task of the day. This first accomplishment gives you a sense of pride that you carry with you to the next task. That one task completed will have turned into many tasks completed by the end of the day. Making your bed also serves as a reminder that the little things matter. And if you can't do the little things right, you won't do the big things right.[84]

Think about the feeling you get after listening to a powerful motivational speech. You walk away feeling motivated, engaged, and ready to take action. It's as if a switch has been turned on and the words you've heard have shifted your perspective.

Motivational speakers are skilled at **activating** their audiences. They are able to switch something on in their audiences that unlocks deep levels of engagement.

Maybe you're thinking, *Do you expect me to be Tony Robbins for my team?* No, you don't need to have a commanding voice and powerful quotes, but what you do need is to have the ability to activate your team.

Activation has to do with flipping the switch, turning on the lightbulb, and providing direction to create a new sense of energy, motivation, and engagement that drives action.

When analyzing how motivational speakers activate an audience, they do three things:

- Connect with the audience
- Provide purpose
- Build self-efficacy

In the third and highest tier in the Hierarchy of Team Engagement Needs, activation consists of those very same characteristics: **connection**, **purpose**, and **belief**. We'll explore each of these in the next three chapters.

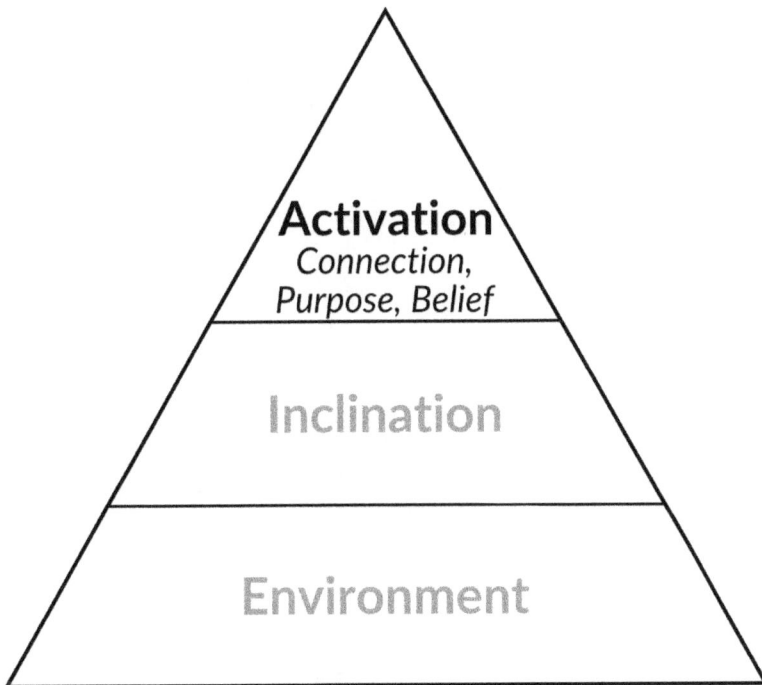

Chapter 14:
Activation—**Connection**

In Denzel Washington's famous "Fail Forward" commencement speech in 2011 at the University of Pennsylvania, before even beginning the script, he first establishes a connection with the audience. He talks about how his son played on the school basketball team and then makes a few jokes about wearing his New York Yankees baseball cap while in Pennsylvania. As he begins the speech, he takes time to reflect on the student experience, the college application experience, and the experience of having been told, "Make sure you have something to fall back on."[85] Why did he spend all that time creating this connection with the audience? He is Denzel Washington, after all. He is a pretty famous and well-known celebrity. He could have spoken of his experience filming his most iconic roles or shared stories from behind the scenes of his most celebrated films. He could have spoken of his Academy Awards, Golden Globe Awards, or Screen Actors Guild Awards. Though all of that would have been impressive and interesting, it would not have created a **connection**.

When a motivational speaker begins a speech, they first make an effort to connect with the audience, building a sense of shared experience and understanding.

From *The Oxford Dictionary*, **con·nec·tion** is defined as "a relationship in which a person, thing, or idea is linked or associated with something else."[86] Feeling connected to someone or something makes an individual feel like they are a part of something else. That positive feeling of connection encourages them to become more attuned to what it is they feel connected to. In Denzel Washington's case, taking the time to establish a connection with the audience made them more receptive to the speech he was about to deliver. All of a sudden, they paid more attention because they felt connected to his experience.

Think about relationships. When you feel connected to your partner, you become more attuned to their thoughts, feelings, and experiences. You pay more attention. You're more receptive. When you feel connected to your family, you share more, you're more understanding, and you're more involved.

Connection is an essential part of activation because it encourages each person to do their part to maintain the relationship.

When we feel connected to our teams, we are more attuned to the collective goals of the team and seek ways to contribute to them.

When we feel disconnected from our team, we don't feel the same obligation to contribute or to attune ourselves to the needs of others.

A Connected Team:	A Disconnected Team:
• Is attuned to one another. • Embraces contribution. • Seeks solutions for the collective. • Makes recommendations to better the team.	• Is attuned to themselves. • Avoids contributions. • Seeks solutions for the individual. • Makes requests for personal gain.

THE IMPACT OF DISCONNECTION

I've worked with a company that saw their team go from connected to disconnected over time. This change was caused by the company's rapid growth and fast-increasing revenue. In an effort to improve efficiency, management implemented a procedure for a step-by-step workflow that dictated how tasks should be completed and clearly defined which steps each department was responsible for. Determined to make it work, management strictly enforced the procedure, ensuring there was no overlap between roles and that employees focused solely on their assigned tasks. Although it improved efficiency, it had an adverse effect. It created silos. The focus changed from completing projects together to competing as individual groups. Each department focused only on steps in the procedure that applied to them, and when things went wrong, it was easy to use the procedure to point fingers at the team who missed a step. Meetings turned into disputes over resources and competitions fueled by the perception of unfair distribution of responsibility in the procedure. People were no longer receptive to the challenges faced by other departments and could not see how these challenges were affecting the company as a whole. Instead, they chose to hold on tightly to their frustrations with one another. Operating with an "us vs. them" mentality, each department focused narrowly on its own procedural responsibilities, and this disconnection led employees to lose sight of the organization's collective goals.

Disconnection is an inevitable team challenge. Without an active effort to create and maintain connection, disconnection is a natural outcome. Similar to our friendships and relationships, without actively trying to create connection, we inevitably feel more disconnected. As disconnection grows, the team members begin to pull back, focusing on their individual challenges and less on the objectives of the team as a whole. Team members begin to contribute less, and discretionary effort declines as the individual team members feel less engaged. In our organizations, there are several situations that contribute to disconnectedness.

- **Difficult Market Conditions**: We're all familiar with the ebbs and flows of economic conditions. For businesses, these changes affect buying behaviour, demand, and supply. Businesses are particularly affected by these changes and are often forced to pivot their business strategy in response. As conditions grow more difficult, pressure to deliver results increases.[87] With rising organizational demands and heightened performance expectations, competitiveness often increases—while connection and collaboration may begin to erode, strained by uncertainty and the fear of job loss. Team members act out of self-preservation, and self-preservation is about saving the *self* and not the team.

- **Organizational Changes**: Organizational changes such as layoffs, restructuring, mergers or acquisitions, or the departure of the founders can disrupt established workflows, causing confusion and disconnection. When new business functions are added or the company scales up, the structure can become more complex as new layers of management are added. Departments can become siloed, focusing on their specific responsibilities and losing sight of the goals of the organization as a whole. Even within departments, team members can become overly focused on the responsibilities outlined in their job descriptions without considering how their contributions impact the team. Instead of being attuned to the team, the individual members are attuned only to their own needs during the change process.

- **Perceived Unimportance of Creating Connection**: Often, changes in leadership bring shifts in perception and priorities. New leaders may feel pressure to demonstrate quick wins and focus on key metrics or performance indicators. As a result, they may unintentionally deprioritize building connection within their team. This lack of connection can cause employees to feel less valued and more like cogs in a machine rather than contributors to a shared goal. Over time, the disconnection will reduce attunement and engagement, ultimately affecting long-term productivity.

- **Unresolved Conflict**: Disagreements are a natural part of working together—we won't always see eye to eye. But when those disagreements escalate into conflict and remain unresolved, they can breed resentment, gradually driving a wedge between team members and weakening connection. Without an active approach to resolving conflict—one that ensures employees feel heard, encourages collaborative problem-solving, and includes intentional efforts to reconnect—disconnection is inevitable.

Regardless of where or how connection is lost, disconnection breeds disengagement. Simply ask yourself: Can you truly feel engaged in something that you're also disconnected from?

As a matter of fact, the rise of *remote* work has raised questions about its potential to contribute to team disconnection.

TO WORK REMOTE OR NOT TO WORK REMOTE: THAT IS THE QUESTION

Following the COVID-19 pandemic of 2019–2021, remote work gained popularity. Many in-office jobs became hybrid or fully remote roles as more organizations invested in virtual conferencing, messaging, and collaboration software tools. Then, between 2023 and 2024, many employers pushed to bring workers back to the office, and the great debate over remote work ensued.

The statistics say that "90% of remote workers report consistent or higher productivity rates working remotely, as compared with in-office work."[88] While this number is self-reported, there are many advantages to remote work for employees and employers.

For employees:

- Yes, it allows employees to skip the office distractions and the water cooler chats to focus on their tasks.
- Yes, it saves time, energy, and money spent on commuting.
- Yes, it contributes to flexibility and work-life balance.

For employers:

- Yes, it saves money on office and utility expenses.[89]
- Yes, it helps save time by reducing interruptions from employees dropping by your desk or office for a chat.
- Yes, it provides access to a wider talent pool.

On the other hand, despite the many virtual collaboration tools, remote work makes **connection** difficult. And it's not just a result of poor internet connection causing pixelated faces or laggy audio. It's the absence of a shared physical space, body language, impromptu casual conversations, and real-time, in-person updates.

In order to activate your team to increase engagement, they need to feel connected. While fully remote work is a barrier to connection, hybrid work could be the answer to taking advantage of the benefits of both remote and in-person work. It allows you to bring the team together for collaboration and make a deliberate effort to foster connection, while also giving them focused time to work on their tasks at home.

The point is that connection should be an active consideration for your team. Connection can get lost in many ways, even in the work structure. However, even in difficult times and in complex industries, leaders like Janet Wardle keep their team connected.

CONNECTION REQUIRES LISTENING, NOT ROCKET SCIENCE

Janet Wardle was the recipient of the 2024 Business Person of the Year Award by the Mississauga Board of Trade, while serving as the president and CEO of MHI Canada Aerospace. This company specializes in the manufacturing of aircraft components and has a team of over 700 people. Even at this scale, Janet focuses on creating an activated team by building connection.

In my interview with Janet, she told me, "It's about making sure people feel like part of a team. When there's a problem, I try to involve as many people as possible, not just a select few, because collaboration is key." It was evident that for her, creating real connection starts with being approachable and breaking down the hierarchy. When people feel safe and seen, they're more likely to engage, share ideas, and speak up.

Janet added, "When I go down to the shop floor, it's not like people scatter. Instead, they come over, eager to tell me what's going on. That's the result of building relationships where they know I'm not someone to be afraid of." Janet believes that every role is essential to moving the boat (or the plane) forward, and it's about ensuring everyone feels equal and understands how their contributions are valuable to the bigger picture.

Connection also means listening, especially when it's inconvenient or uncomfortable. It's easy to dismiss frustration when solutions aren't obvious, but taking the time to understand where someone is coming from changes everything. "For example, during COVID, many of us in the office worked from home, while the people on the shop floor still had to be there in person. I'd get notes from them saying, 'Janet, we want to work from home too,' and I'd think, 'How am I supposed to move the aircraft wing from one house to another? Let's be realistic!' But instead of dismissing them, I'd respond with empathy. I'd acknowledge their frustration and say, 'I know it's tough wearing masks and safety glasses all day in this heat. But let's work through this together.' Even when their requests seemed impractical, I made sure they knew I understood where they were coming from."

Janet prioritized connection on her team because she understood that without it, you miss out on the benefits of high levels of engagement. Listening is just one way to create connection. There are several other ways to build connection on your team, and fortunately, they are also not rocket science.

Pro Tips: How to Establish Connection

Just like building relationships, creating a sense of connectedness within your team takes time and consistent effort. The goal is to ensure that every member of your team feels like they belong. Here are some ways to approach this.

Build "Community"

I have always found the dynamics in hair salons and barbershops very interesting. Besides the diverse clientele, bringing a mixture of unique personalities, the dynamics between the hair stylists and the barbers are also interesting. I've visited salons where the stylists are clearly disconnected from one another. The tension in the air is thick, and I've even been privy to some of the gossip while in the chair. In contrast, I've also been to salons where there was a sense of connection, giving it a family-oriented feel. The stylists communicated well, shared laughs, and genuinely seemed to enjoy being in each other's presence.

At one such hair salon, I interviewed the owner, Alicia Gibson, and asked how she keeps her staff engaged and fosters this sense of connection. She said, "I prioritize the 3Cs. Consistency, communication, and community." When I asked her what community meant to her, she said, "Community for me is cultivating a space where people feel connected to one another. That means that they feel safe, supported, and heard. It's about a sense of togetherness where they feel like they belong and want to contribute to what we are creating."

"How do you create that?" I asked. She explained, "The first two Cs, consistency and communication, are essential for building strong relationships and provide the foundation for community. A true sense of community goes deeper. It's about the positivity you bring, the enthusiasm you share, the way you cheer each other on, and the openness to accept people for who they are. Most importantly, it's about having empathy for one other and recognizing each other's unique experiences so that we all feel valued."

Remember Surprises Aren't Always Fun

Have you ever had a friend call you on the phone with a surprising decision about something you had no previous knowledge of? Perhaps you felt blindsided because this decision seemingly came out of nowhere? Your first thought is likely, *Whoa, where is all this coming from?* As their friend, you would have expected to have been privy to the thought process that led up to this big decision, so it would not have come as such a shock. Instead, you're left wondering why your friend chose not to bring you into the loop earlier. You might even begin to question your relationship.

Now imagine that a big decision is made by the management team to launch a new service. As the leader, you come to share the news with the team, and they don't seem overly excited about the decision. When you ask for their feedback, they say that this service is not what the customers are looking for. Your team is in contact with the customers daily and know the nuances of their needs. Making a decision without consulting the very people who have the closest relationship with the customers is the exact opposite of feeling connected. What your team feels at these moments is blindsided, left out, and undervalued.

Many strategic decisions in organizations are made behind closed doors. Then, it's up to the managers to disseminate the details about the decision amongst their teams. The problem is that these decisions often come as a surprise to the team members, and it's rarely a fun experience for them. Sometimes, feeling connected is as simple as feeling involved. When we involve our team in decision-making, progress, and results, they feel connected to and invested in the process. This will encourage them to share feedback and ideas that may be beneficial to the team and also supports their buy-in and engagement with implementation.

Keeping a transparent flow of communication among your team keeps surprises at bay. I have worked with several companies looking for support in their change management process. The common denominator between all these teams undergoing change is that they feel a sense of disconnection and broken communication. The costs are high when change efforts go wrong—not only financially but in confusion, lost opportunity, wasted resources, and diminished morale.[90] Principles of effective change management include involving your people early in the process and throughout the process, and providing transparent communication.

At one company I've worked with, teams had two daily touchpoint meetings: one in the morning and one after lunch. They were usually less than ten minutes, but each person shared updates on what they were working on and the challenges they were facing. It was an opportunity to share ideas or offer a helping hand if someone needed one. It was also an opportunity for managers to set priorities or redistribute the work if needed. The team was highly connected because of the transparency and awareness of what was in the pipeline and how closely the team collaborated with the managers. There were no surprises here.

And don't forget to:

- **Be Cautious of Translucence**: Sometimes, as leaders, it is considered strategic to withhold certain information. Be cautious when you do this. Your team may be able to sense that there is more to the story. When your team sees the whole picture, they are more likely to trust and align with the direction. When they know that you're withholding information, they might focus more on what they don't know rather than what they do, leading to speculation, suspicion, and feelings of disconnectedness.
- **Be Sure You Listen**: Encouraging feedback and creating communication channels requires that you listen. As the leader, you may not always agree with or like what you hear, but shutting down ideas

or getting defensive will slow your team's willingness to share feedback.

Send an Invitation

Have you ever received an invitation to an event and felt surprised because you didn't think you were close enough to make the guest list?

Between 2022 and 2023, I attended fourteen weddings. Yes, fourteen. Many of them were for close friends of mine, but others were for friends with whom I had grown distant. I noticed that although many times I found myself surprised to be invited, I was also honoured. It had me reflecting on the relationships we had and recalling the positive moments we shared. If they wanted my presence on their special day, then I must be special to them. Suddenly, I felt more connected to these people, just because of an invitation.

As leaders, sometimes we focus only on what has to be done. All that is mandatory. It could be the client meetings, team meetings, work-related check-ins, and performance reviews. These are the events where the members of your team are "required" attendees. But what about the instances where their attendance is optional? This could be a project meeting a team member might find interesting, a networking event your organization got invited to, or perhaps a webinar that you think your team might find valuable. Extending invitations to your team for non-mandatory events or opportunities that are beneficial or enjoyable makes them feel valued, appreciated, and wanted, creating a sense of connection. It's the moments where they know that you *didn't have to, but you did* anyway. It shows that you were thinking of them beyond their mandatory duties and that you care. Just be sure to distribute the invitations evenly across your team so that no one feels left out or overlooked!

Organize Regular Team-Building Events

Don't roll your eyes. Yes, team building has developed a negative reputation. To employees and managers, it often comes across as a series of embarrassing and irrelevant activities like hula hooping, tug-of-war, or a three-legged race. These activities are often perceived as a waste of time and ineffective at building team connection. It's unfortunate that team building has gotten a bad rap because team building is truly a powerful tool for improving workplace dynamics, as long as it is done right.

In order to be done right, team-building events should be:

- Meaningful
- Fun
- Regular

Team-building events should be designed to break down the barriers between your team members. It requires a thoughtful look at what is standing in the way of their connection. If the activities are designed arbitrarily, they will feel arbitrary and artificial. However, if you create meaningful activities, you'll get a better outcome.

For example, if your team's barriers to connection lie in their:

Problem-Solving Difficulty	Run problem-solving scenarios, such as escape room challenges, survival scenario challenges, or strategy sessions.
Understanding	Run exercises that encourage the understanding of a new perspective, such as fun role-reversal challenges, charades, personality type showdowns (taking personality tests and then completing activities), or even tours (museum tours, food tours, historical site tours, etc.).
Communication	Run activities that rely on communication, such as blindfolded challenges, group storytelling, or fun team debates.
Social Hesitation / Reluctance	Run activities that get them out of their comfort zones, such as improv comedy, adventure challenges (ziplining, rock climbing), or obstacle courses.

Whatever you choose, the activities should be selected meaningfully.

These activities should also be fun. They should not feel like work. Activities that explicitly aim to drive home some sort of lesson or teach workplace-specific skills often lose their impact. The learning should occur naturally and subtly through the experience. Having the team spend time together, sharing an experience, learning or working together towards a common goal allows bonding to happen more organically and far more effectively.[91]

Most team building falls flat because many organizations schedule them as a one-time activity. However, team building is most effective when it is ongoing. It should be used as a tool to keep the excitement and the connection alive. In a *Forbes* article, Brian Scudamore, the founder of the well-known brand 1-800-GOT-JUNK? mentions that team building is the most important investment you can make for your people.[92] He says that effective team building means more engaged employees, which is good for company culture and boosting the bottom line. It doesn't always have to be fancy, but an investment in ongoing team building is worthwhile. Perhaps one month you choose a unique experience like a cooking class or a camping trip and other months you might have a quick huddle with a "one thing you don't know about me," a show and tell, or an appreciation circle. You'll know you got it right when there is a sense of excitement, a sense of accomplishment, and more connection.

A connected team sparks individual engagement and drives collective effort. A connection is what activates each member to contribute and invest their discretionary effort into the team. It encourages better performance because it makes people care to do better not for themselves but for the team. Upon connection, the next need for activation is providing a strong guiding force for where that team is going. In other words, purpose.

Chapter 15:
Activation—**Purpose**

To generate extraordinary profits, you must first have a focus that is beyond profits.

— Punit Renjen, former CEO of Deloitte

Bill Hewlett and Dave Packard met at Stanford University in the 1930s, where they studied engineering. While living together in 1938 in Palo Alto, California, they spent a lot of time tinkering and building in their garage workshop. They worked on prototypes for inventions and made their first breakthrough with an audio-oscillator device that measured sound frequencies, which they named the 200A. Their efforts gained momentum when they sold audio oscillators to Walt Disney Studios, which used them for the movie *Fantasia*. Following this success, they formalized their partnership on January 1, 1939, and Hewlett-Packard (HP) was born.[93]

Today HP is a multinational information technology company that sells hardware, software, and related business services. They are regarded as the founding Silicon Valley company and pioneers of "The HP Way." As the company grew from a garage start-up into a large organization, Bill and Dave faced a dilemma familiar to many Silicon Valley founders today: how to step back and allow the business to grow and thrive without micromanaging every detail.

Dave Packard would later say: "Early in our history, while thinking about how the company should be managed, I kept getting back to one concept: If we simply got everyone to agree on what our objectives were, then we could just provide them with the right conditions and resources and turn them all loose and they would all move along in a common **direction**."[94] Bill and Dave gave their growing team a clear purpose to guide their action.

When the purpose is clear, there is a pronounced guideline for action and decision-making.

TEAMS NEED PURPOSE

Can you recall a time when you felt so moved by a cause that you decided to participate? I recently came across a charitable organization called Courage in Action, whose purpose activated me. The mission statement reads: "To bring women together to inspire confidence, foster friendships, and teach life skills as they move from adversity to possibility." As I read more, I felt moved by the stories and testimonials of the women who had found the courage and the support they needed in some of the most difficult times in their lives. When I discovered they were seeking volunteer facilitators to lead programs aimed at improving these women's lives, I signed up without hesitation. I saw the purpose and was compelled to contribute to it. And I knew exactly how to do that.

By definition, a team is a group of people working together with shared goals. When you remove the shared goals, you remove the purpose of the team, and instead, you've just got a group of people.

Where are we going?
Why are we here?
What are we supposed to do?

These questions, even if they are merely thoughts, indicate that the purpose of the team is unclear. Whether you refer to them as goals, objectives, direction, or purpose, these are all variations of the same fundamental concept. They answer the questions: *Where are we going? Why are we here? And what are we supposed to do?* Purpose is about guiding action. Similar to a destination on a map, if the team knows what the purpose is, they can distinguish between what action will move them in the right direction and what action won't. Without that purpose, team members might find themselves moving in different directions, struggling to coordinate and streamline their efforts. **When purpose is unclear, action is misguided.**

If you aim at nothing, you'll hit it every time.—Zig Ziglar

Once the purpose is made clear, the more meaningful and compelling it is, the stronger the activation in your team. This activation manifests as a strong desire and motivation to take the necessary action to fulfill the purpose. Purpose *engages* a team in the process of its fulfillment. That engagement through purpose has a clear correlation to performance and profitability, as team members are motivated to do their very best and fulfill the purpose as efficiently and effectively as possible.

PURPOSE AND PERFORMANCE

Marta Gnatek is the director of client services and executive search at Creative Niche. Creative Niche is an award-winning recruitment agency specializing in marketing, account service, design, strategy, creative, and digital. Marta has led a successful career in human resources and has specialized in recruitment for over ten years. Given her diverse understanding of employee-employer relations across sectors and organizations, I wanted to know her thoughts on employee engagement needs.

She shared, "The most important thing is that employees feel connected to the purpose and mission of the organization. Employees should have a clear understanding of the correlation between their roles, the impact they have, and the overall organizational goals. They need to be able to see how their work contributes to something meaningful. At Creative Niche, our purpose is to connect great talent with great employers. I live and breathe this every day by getting to know people and their career goals and understanding what type of environment would work best for them. I am excited about making the successful match and seeing both the candidate and hiring manager happy. In my work, I directly see the result of my contribution to our organizational purpose, and it keeps me deeply engaged." This clear sense of purpose at Creative Niche contributes to performance. The company, with a strong sense of purpose, boasts a 97% success rate with over 15,000 placements.[95]

Fred Kiel at KRW International, a global consulting firm, completed a research study where he interviewed eighty-four CEOs and their executive teams in-depth (while also doing a poll on 8,600 employees). The study was aimed at quantifying the relationship between CEO character and business success. The results revealed that CEOs who rated high on authentic purpose and values achieved a 9.35% return on assets (net operating income as a proportion of total assets), while self-focused leaders scored just 1.93%. The research showed that the companies run by purpose-driven leaders outperformed self-focused leaders by more than five times.[96]

Employees engaged by a sense of purpose are far more committed to achieving the shared goals of the organization. When your team is invested in the purpose, they go from thinking about simply completing their responsibilities to thinking about how they can make the most meaningful difference. One is about checking a box, while the other engages the employees in ways they can make a positive impact. That positive impact is seen in their resourcefulness and the ways they go above and beyond for clients. In turn, it drives the success of the team and the organization.

An engaged workforce will drive a positive bottom line.
—Marta Gnatek, Creative Niche

To further illustrate just how much of an impact purpose can make, we can look to dragon boat racing.

ONE BOAT, ONE PURPOSE

In university, one of my classmates was on the dragon boat team. Many times, she encouraged me to come and try the sport, but I was hesitant that my lack of experience and historically poor performance on the rowing machine at the gym would disappoint the team. Nonetheless, I remain thoroughly impressed with dragon boating, and even more so because of its relevance to team performance.

If you're unfamiliar with dragon boat racing, it is a competitive water sport where teams, usually consisting of eight to twenty-six people (depending on the boat size), sit in pairs and paddle together in a long, narrow boat known as a dragon boat. What's interesting are the roles.

Each dragon boat has:

- **A Drummer**: A person at the bow (front) of the boat who gives commands and beats the drum, which sets the team's pace.
- **A Steers / Steersperson**: The person at the stern (back) of the boat responsible for steering and giving commands.[97]
- **Paddlers**

If you notice, on that one small dragon boat, both the drummer and the steersperson provide direction.

In all racing sports, the weight of the vehicle / vessel is extremely important to speed. So, for a small boat to accommodate two non-paddling positions, it suggests that their functions are very important. The lesson? Ensuring everyone is aligned in the right direction is more important than maximizing speed. Two people on one boat are responsible for ensuring the team is clear on where they are going and how they should get there. Maximizing performance is not just about paddling as hard as you can. In dragon boating, if team members paddle too hard, it could lead them to fall out of sync with each other. Without proper synchronization, the boat could lose speed and stability, become unbalanced, and potentially start swaying or even tip over. Excessive force could also cause paddlers to burn out prematurely.

In a race, pacing is critical, and paddling too hard can reduce endurance. Maintaining a consistent and coordinated pace with the rest of the team is crucial for maximum efficiency and speed. To win the race, it is more important that the team follows direction and does so in unison. Maintaining a consistent and coordinated pace is what ensures maximum performance. The leader (or leaders) must make this direction very clear so that everyone understands exactly what they need to do and how it contributes to where they're going.

If you want your team to win the race, ask yourself: Have I clearly communicated the direction and purpose? Does everyone understand their role and how it contributes to reaching the goal? If the team falls out of sync, is there a way to get them back on beat?

Although there is a **shared team purpose**, each team member will have a different reason for being a part of it. In other words, their **personal purpose** is unique.

SHARED PURPOSE VS. PERSONAL PURPOSE

On a dragon boat racing team, the goal is very clear: to win the race, of course. Although everyone on the team is there to do their part to win that race, they may want to win for different reasons:

- Some may be seeking the self-esteem and personal satisfaction that comes from achieving a difficult goal.
- Some may seek validation from family, peers, or mentors who are watching their performance.
- Some may view winning as a stepping stone to opening doors for other opportunities.
- Some may be driven by the thrill and excitement of the competition itself.
- Some may be seeking to belong on a winning team.
- And some may be interested in leaving a lasting impact or creating a legacy that will be remembered.

Drawing the connection between personal purpose and shared purpose creates activation. It answers the "What's in it for me?" (WIIFM) principle in a profound way. It's the difference between saying "Let's win this dragon boat race!" and "Let's win this dragon boat race so that your parents can see how hard you've worked when you cross the finish line!" Or "Let's win this dragon boat race so that we go down in history as the regional champions! We will have the opportunity to compete at the world level!"

Leaning on personal purpose is especially important when an organization's shared purpose is not compelling enough on its own. For example, the vision statement of the Royal Bank of Canada (RBC) reads: "To be among the world's most trusted and successful financial institutions."[98] What's in it for the team? What about that purpose is activating the team? What's in it for them (WIIFT)? Instead, if leaders tied this shared purpose to their team's personal purpose, it would be more activating: "We're working on becoming the most successful financial institution where we can also create the most success in your life, with career growth, financial benefits, and helping you fulfill your potential." This highlights what's in it for them.

Team members are most engaged when their personal purpose can be fulfilled while they pursue the team's shared goals. Most importantly, however, that purpose must be meaningful.

Don't Forget to Make It Meaningful

It's tempting to rely on short-term incentives—like bonuses or rewards—to answer the WIIFM question and give your team a sense of personal purpose while they work towards the shared purpose. Offering incentives can be effective for sparking initial motivation or activating your team towards a goal. However, this approach only works in the short term. Sustained engagement requires activating your team with a purpose that is deeply *meaningful to them*. To some, that certainly may be financial rewards, though to others, it may be making an impact in their own way, fulfilling their potential or accomplishing a personal goal.

While a meaningful purpose is powerful in activating your team, accountability is also necessary to keep them on track and optimize their performance.

ACCOUNTABILITY

The most common New Year's resolutions are fitness goals. Yet, according to a study by the University of Scranton, 92% of people fail to achieve their New Year's resolutions.[99] In January, the fitness gyms are filled. By February, the gym population has thinned out, and by March, only the regular gym crowd remains. Why is it so hard for people to stay on track if the goal is clear and the purpose is compelling and meaningful?

Well, why does working with a personal trainer significantly increase the likelihood of achieving fitness goals?

Because, in the pursuit of personal purpose or shared purpose, **accountability** is key.

In addition to keeping clients on track for their goals, a personal trainer will make adjustments to strategy and form to make their efforts more effective. Teams require the same accountability to support their performance. Just as a driver steers a vehicle to keep it from drifting out of its lane, accountability ensures the team stays on course, even when the direction is clear.

Think back to dragon boat racing, where the drummer plays a key role in accountability. Keeping the paddlers on pace so that they don't drift is important in maintaining the overall performance of the team. Although the team may intuitively know when to paddle harder or slower, the rhythm of the drumbeat holds them accountable to a specific standard of performance and makes it more likely that they fulfill their purpose.

Pro Tips: How to Activate Your Team with Purpose

Giving your team purpose gives them the direction and clarity they need to guide their action. It allows them to understand the results and the impact of their contribution. Purpose helps your team stay engaged in the process of accomplishing it. When activating your team with purpose, keep in mind these three principles:

- **Clarity**: Ensure the shared purpose is clearly understood. Be transparent with your team about what you are trying to accomplish and why. Help them understand the impact.

- **Link Shared Purpose with Personal Purpose**: Especially when shared purpose is not compelling enough on its own, help employees understand what's in it for them (WIIFT) by tying the shared purpose to something personal and meaningful to them.

- **Accountability**: Keep the team accountable to the purpose. It keeps them from veering off course. Keep the team on track with milestones and regular check-ins to ensure their efforts and focus are on the activities that contribute to the shared purpose or team goals.

With a sense of connection and a compelling purpose guiding the team in the right direction, the last element for activation is belief.

Chapter 16:
Activation—**Belief**

Whether you think you can, or you think you can't—you're right.
—Henry Ford

In the sixth instalment of the iconic Harry Potter film series, there is a scene where one of the main characters, Ron Weasley, is nervous about his upcoming Quidditch (a fictional sport) match. So doubtful of his ability, he mentions quitting the team and giving up his spot for someone else. The title character, Harry Potter, pretends to pour a magic potion, "Liquid Luck," into his drink to give him good luck for the game. As a result of the placebo, Ron's belief in his ability to perform manifests into an exceptional game-winning performance.[100]

The placebo effect is so strong because the power of **belief** is strong. Our belief about what is possible often determines exactly what is possible *for us*.

The limit of performance is equal to the limit of belief.

When looking at belief as a key component of activation and engagement, it's important to assess three things:

- The team's belief in themselves (self-efficacy)
- The leader's belief in the team
- Shared beliefs

No matter how much effort you put into improving team engagement and performance, your efforts will be undermined by the team's lack of belief in their potential, your lack of belief in their potential, or shared beliefs that are detrimental to your goals.

THE TEAM'S BELIEF IN THEMSELVES (SELF-EFFICACY THEORY)

A person's belief in their ability to succeed in a particular situation is referred to as self-efficacy. This concept was first introduced in 1977 by social-cognitive psychologist Albert Bandura.

Self-efficacy has an unconscious yet very strong connection to engagement. Bandura proposed that self-efficacy influences the activities people choose to engage in, the amount of effort they invest, how long they persist in the face of challenges, and their overall performance. Compared to individuals with high self-doubt, those with strong self-efficacy tend to engage more actively, put in greater effort, persist through challenges, and ultimately achieve higher levels of success.[101] Self-efficacy, therefore, is directly linked to engagement. For those with low self-efficacy, or the belief that they cannot successfully complete the task at hand, the natural response is to disengage or avoid the task. If you believe that a successful outcome is impossible, what's the point of trying? Putting in extra effort seems pointless when you're up against something that is seemingly impossible. In contrast, those with high self-efficacy firmly believe that success is not only possible but within their control. They actively engage in the process and are psychologically equipped to overcome challenges in order to succeed. Their confidence lies in the belief that a solution exists and that they simply need to figure it out.

A team with high self-efficacy that has been put in the right environment and aligned in their inclination will naturally be higher performing. However, measures of self-efficacy and self-doubt can be difficult to quantify. A team with high levels of self-doubt may still achieve goals and fulfill objectives; however, the way in which they do so will likely be slower and less innovative than teams with high levels of self-efficacy. What you will see are the warning signs of the hindrances of low self-efficacy.

The indicators that self-efficacy is low include:

- **Unconfident Language**: "Well, I guess I'll try, but I can't promise anything."
- **Lack of Enthusiasm**: "I guess we have to do this."
- **Pushback on Goals**: "Maybe we should aim for something more achievable."
- **Negative Feedback**: "This will never work." "I knew this was going to fall apart."

The indicators that self-efficacy is high are the opposite:

- **Confident Language**: "Absolutely, and maybe we should even..."
- **Enthusiasm**: "I'm really excited about the impact this project could have!"
- **Resilience**: "Setbacks are a part of the process. What if we tried it this way instead?" "Let's tweak it and try again."
- **Encouraging Feedback**: "What a great idea!" "What great work you did; we can build on that!"

Many factors contribute to self-efficacy or a team's belief in their own ability. One of those factors is whether the **leader** believes in their ability.

THE LEADER'S BELIEF IN THE TEAM (THE PYGMALION EFFECT)

In 1965, Robert Rosenthal of Harvard conducted an experiment where he administered an IQ test to all the students in a California elementary school. Without revealing the results, Rosenthal told the elementary school teachers that some of their new students were extremely intelligent and had extraordinary potential. In reality, these students were selected at random and had no identified extraordinary abilities.

At the end of the school year, Rosenthal administered the IQ test again, and the students who were initially categorized as more talented had significantly increased their performance compared to the rest of the class. Rosenthal concluded that just the expectation of certain behaviours leads us to act in ways that make the expected behaviour more likely to occur. This is what is known as the Pygmalion effect, the phenomenon in which expectations influence the outcome of performance.[102]

In Rosenthal's experiment, the teachers' expectations of high potential in certain students likely influenced how they interacted with them through increased attention, more opportunities, and greater encouragement. Simply believing that your team has the potential to accomplish great things will shift you into becoming an investor in their success.

Believe They Can Fly and They Will

When people are engaged, the results aren't linear—they're exponential. —Kyle Steward

Kyle Steward is a seasoned leader in sales and business development, with extensive experience driving growth across complex industries. He currently serves as director of business development at FBT Inc., a precision manufacturer specializing in advanced manufacturing solutions for sectors including military and defence, energy, and nuclear. With experience managing and growing multimillion-dollar sales portfolios and collaborating with national sales teams, I was eager to hear his perspective on how engagement contributed to the success of business development. He said:

> "I hate to sound trite, but building an engaged team starts with belief. It's saying, 'I believe in you to make decisions, contribute ideas, and make a difference.' But belief alone is not enough. People also need to know precisely what's expected of them—their roles, responsibilities, targets, and how they connect to the bigger mission. Set people up to win. Train them properly, arm them with the necessary tools, and then let them run.

> The best way I've seen it done is when sales and business development teams were treated like entrepreneurs inside the business. Like an investor in a start-up, leadership must first *believe* in the entrepreneur and then support them in their success.

> In the best example I've seen, new hires didn't just sit through a death-by-PowerPoint onboarding. They got real coaching: building a territory plan, leading value-driven conversations, and owning the

customer relationship from hello to handshake. Their roles and responsibilities were clear. Not in corporate buzzword bingo, but in real, practical terms: Here's what success looks like, here's how it ties to the bigger picture, and here's how we'll help you get there. They were given frameworks—flexible enough to encourage curiosity, creativity, and professional judgment. Recognition wasn't reserved for the end-of-year party either. Wins were celebrated. Losses were studied, not punished. And the result of leadership's belief in their team? People acted like owners. They didn't wait for permission. They built trust with customers, found hidden opportunities, and believed in what they were selling. Engagement wasn't a quarterly initiative or a buzzword on a PowerPoint. It was what happened when people were believed in, trained, and treated like professionals.

Now, I've seen the opposite too. New hires dumped into two hours of onboarding, handed a stale list of cold leads (if they even got that), given a number to hit without a plan, and left to figure it out. Leadership only showed up when numbers slipped. Wins were ignored. Losses were punished. Compensation plans were changed midstream without transparency or logic, eroding trust one bad decision at a time. No ownership. No coaching. No connection to purpose. Just pressure without partnership. And here's what happens: The best people check out, or they walk out. Then, management blames 'bad hires' instead of broken systems.

Why is belief important? Because it creates engaged teams. And poor engagement doesn't just hurt culture; it kills your pipeline before it even has a chance to grow."[103]

In addition to a leader's belief in their team and one's belief in themselves, *shared beliefs* are the unwritten and invisible guiding principles of a group of people.

SHARED BELIEFS

If you boarded a flight in North America in the 1980s, not only would you have been squeezing by other passengers' baggage while trying to find your seat, but you would have also been squinting through clouds of smoke. Smoking cigarettes was allowed on airplanes up until the 1990s. Today, that seems asinine, not only because of the health consequences but also the potential dangers of open flames on a small metal tube 35,000 feet in the air. But at the time, the shared beliefs around smoking, even on airplanes, were different.

Before that, in the 1960s, tobacco consumption was at its peak popularity. This was all driven by advertising campaigns that shaped shared beliefs. Tobacco companies advertised smoking as a symbol of sophistication, glamour, and even health. Celebrities also appeared in these ad campaigns, endorsing cigarettes. At one point, doctors were even hired to market tobacco, as companies used slogans like "Just What the Doctor Ordered" and "More Doctors Smoke Camels."[104]

The entire advertising industry is built on creating shared beliefs in order to drive behaviour (typically purchasing behaviour) because creating a belief is far more effective than making a request or issuing a command. The same is true for our teams.

Belief drives behaviour, and behaviour drives results...or lack thereof.

Shared Beliefs Drive Action, but They Also Drive Inaction.

At its peak in September 2011, there were 85 million BlackBerry smartphone users worldwide.[105] BlackBerry Limited (formerly Research in Motion) was known for bringing innovative products to the market. They pioneered bringing email services to handheld mobile devices with a QWERTY keyboard. The widespread adoption of their devices by business professionals led to wild success. Then, in 2007, Apple launched the iPhone. The shared belief at BlackBerry was that the iPhone was just an enhanced mobile phone with playful features targeted at younger consumers.[106] This belief caused company-wide inaction.

Contrary to their beliefs, the iPhone offered more than just email and messaging capabilities. Through the "App Store," Apple brought multimedia experiences to consumers and created an all-in-one tool and entertainment hub through the phone. Again, BlackBerry's beliefs about what consumers needed caused their inaction to respond to what consumers wanted. With these beliefs, BlackBerry chose to focus on its traditional strengths. They failed to invest in a robust "app" ecosystem and ignored the growing demand for better cameras, social media integration, and multimedia capabilities.[107] This led to the downfall of BlackBerry smartphones.

Beliefs have a powerful influence on our outcomes, good or bad. Activating your team with powerful beliefs will deeply engage them in a course of action. That depth of engagement has infinite possibilities.

Pro Tips: Activating Your Team with Shared Beliefs

A powerful leader can **activate** their team by creating a shared belief. That activation sparks positive action. For instance:

- A team with a shared belief that customer experience is paramount will prioritize the customer experience and make decisions that improve customer experience.
- A team with a shared belief that innovation is the priority will look for ways to innovate in all that they do.
- A team with a shared belief that customer education is important will spend additional time educating customers about their solution.

The advertising industry uses three key principles in creating shared beliefs that can also be applied to teams: **repetition, consistency,** and **proof.** We're bombarded by repeated messages that remain consistent no matter through which channel they are received. Those messages are often accompanied by proof, whether social proof, customer reviews, guarantees, or endorsements from figures of authority. These principles are what form our beliefs about brands, which ultimately determine our economic behaviour.

On our teams, we can apply these principles to create beliefs that impact engagement behaviour.

Repetition: Reinforce Key Messages

The Rule of 7 is a marketing principle that states that customers need to see a message at least seven times before they commit to a purchase decision.[108] Sending one message to your team is not enough. They will forget. They're human. Repeating the message is necessary for retention. The more the message is repeated, the more it is reinforced and internalized as a belief.

In practice, this might look like:

- Regularly repeating core messages during meetings, through written communications and in one-on-one discussions.
- Repeatedly telling stories and sharing examples that reflect the team's shared beliefs.

Consistency: Model and Maintain Standards

In order to create a shared belief, the team needs to see consistency with what they're told, what they observe, and what the company does. If these do not align, the belief will quickly be dissolved with doubt.

For example, I've seen leaders who tout company policies as imperative guidelines that all team members must follow. Then comes a difficult customer challenging a team member about the policies. The customer asks, "Can I speak to a manager?" Instead of reinforcing the belief that policies cannot be broken, the manager says, "This time, we will make an exception." In that very instant, the team member's beliefs about the importance of the policies are shattered. How important could the policies be if they were so easily broken to appease this customer? The messaging is inconsistent.

Ensuring the message is consistent through all channels is important to create confidence and reliability in the shared belief system.

In practice, this means:

- The message is consistent and clear across all channels.
- Leaders model behaviour that supports the message or the shared beliefs. They lead by example. They do not say one thing and then do another.
- The same standards are applied consistently to all team members and situations.

Proof: Show Outcomes of Beliefs

In a world full of ads and people trying to convince us or sell us something, we've all become a little skeptical. We need proof to back up claims. Proof provides validation. When team members see the impact of shared beliefs, they are more likely to buy into them. For example, Palantir Technologies, a company specializing in software platforms for big data analytics, believes in having their engineers do the tasks that a traditional sales team would do. Their unconventional belief was that they should hire no salespeople. They simply sent in their engineers to speak about the product and how it was built. At first, employees, specifically engineers who now have sales tasks, were shocked by this, but once they saw the positive results of focusing on client education, they were fully on board and far more engaged in partnering with (rather than selling to) their clients.[109]

Proof can come in many forms; it doesn't need to be data organized in the form of charts and tables. In fact, most marketing initiatives rely heavily on social proof, testimonials, or the experiences of others. When was the last time you checked the reviews before buying something online?

In practice, this means:

- Sharing data or success stories that confirm and validate the team's beliefs. For example, share customer feedback that illustrates how a shared belief led to improved project outcomes.
- Recognizing and celebrating behaviours that align with the shared beliefs. This serves as positive reinforcement, associating positive outcomes with the shared beliefs.
- Creating opportunities for social proof where team members can share their own proof of how those shared beliefs have led to positive outcomes.

People are deeply motivated to act according to the things they believe in. They are also very reluctant to act when they don't believe in something. Therefore, creating strong *shared beliefs* supported by the *expectation of positive outcomes* and *self-efficacy* on your team creates a team that is highly activated and engaged to perform.

An activated team, in other words, a **connected** group of people with **shared beliefs** around a common **purpose**, will find deep levels of engagement that allow them to tap into the highest levels of performance.

Activation Key Takeaways: Where There's Activation, There's a Way

In the Hierarchy of Team Engagement Needs, the third and final tier—activation—unlocks our deepest level of engagement and performance. Yes, the right environment promotes high performance, and inclination enables that performance, but activation drives the desire for high performance. If we are *connected* to our team, have a compelling *purpose,* and *believe* that it is possible, our engagement is activated. Through activation, we become deeply invested in the outcome. Our role on the team becomes more than a job; it becomes a mission that we are committed to pursuing.

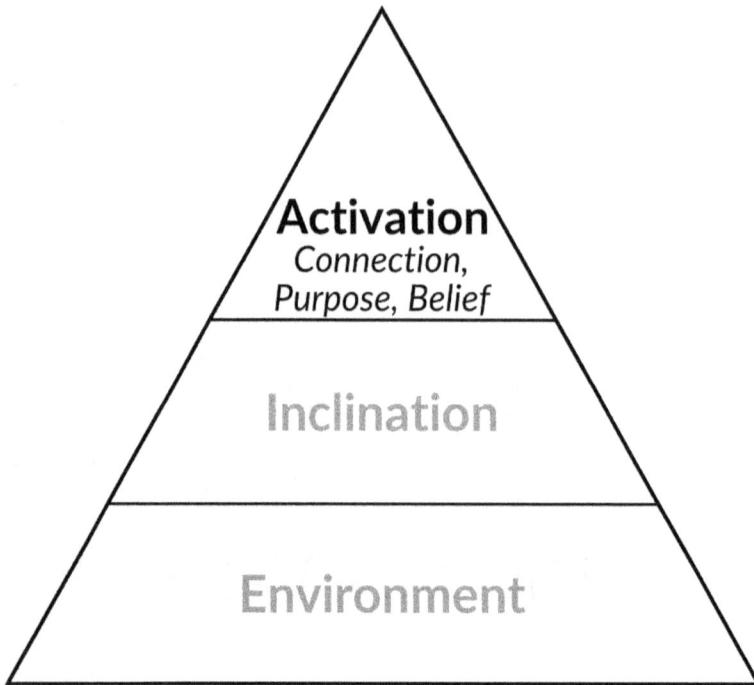

In the last 100 years, when you think of the most remarkable human accomplishments, the 1969 Apollo 11 lunar landing mission can certainly be considered peak human performance. Activation was a large part of that. The pressure was on as the United States and the Soviet Union battled for technological superiority in the Space Race of the 1950s and 1960s.[110] What began with launching satellites into space became a race to the moon when President John F. Kennedy raised the stakes with his "We choose to go to the moon" speech in 1962. He declared:

> "We choose to go to the moon in this decade and do the other things not because they are easy but because they are hard. Because that goal will serve to organize and measure the best of our energies and skills because that challenge is one that we're willing to accept. One we are unwilling to postpone. And one we intend to win."[111]

What happened next was an incredible example of how activation can create the deepest levels of engagement and highest levels of performance.

In order for NASA to successfully land a man on the moon and win the Space Race, it required a team of inclined people—scientists, engineers, mechanics, technicians, pilots, and many more highly skilled people—working together.[112] During a time of much change and uncertainty, Apollo 11 connected people. A sense of national pride, a common opponent (the Soviet Union), and a common **purpose** created a strong **connection** among the team. All those involved embraced their contributions, sought solutions, and worked tirelessly towards their goal. They **believed** that they could achieve the impossible, something that had never been done before. But where there's activation, there's a way. In 1969, Neil Armstrong and Edwin "Buzz" Aldrin stepped foot on the moon. Apollo 11 was the first Apollo mission to attempt a *crewed* lunar landing. On that first attempt, NASA was successful.[113]

An investment in activation will allow your team to reach new heights (pun intended). Through activation, you internalize the team mission as your own mission. When a team is activated, the team's mission doesn't just feel like a directive; it becomes personal. They internalize that mission as their own, fueling their actions with meaning, ownership, and a drive that goes beyond obligation. Activation calls for a sense of connection, a sense of purpose, and belief in the possibility of the desired outcome. The stronger the sense of connection, purpose, and belief, the more deeply activated a team is.

Activated teams require less oversight and management. Activation transforms work into a calling and collaboration into a shared journey towards something greater. When activation sits atop a foundation of environment and inclination, in other words, when all layers of the Hierarchy of Team Engagement Needs are satisfied, the possibilities for performance and profitability (the results of positive engagement economics) are truly endless.

But where do you start when assessing your team's engagement? Next, we'll look at a self-reflection guide.

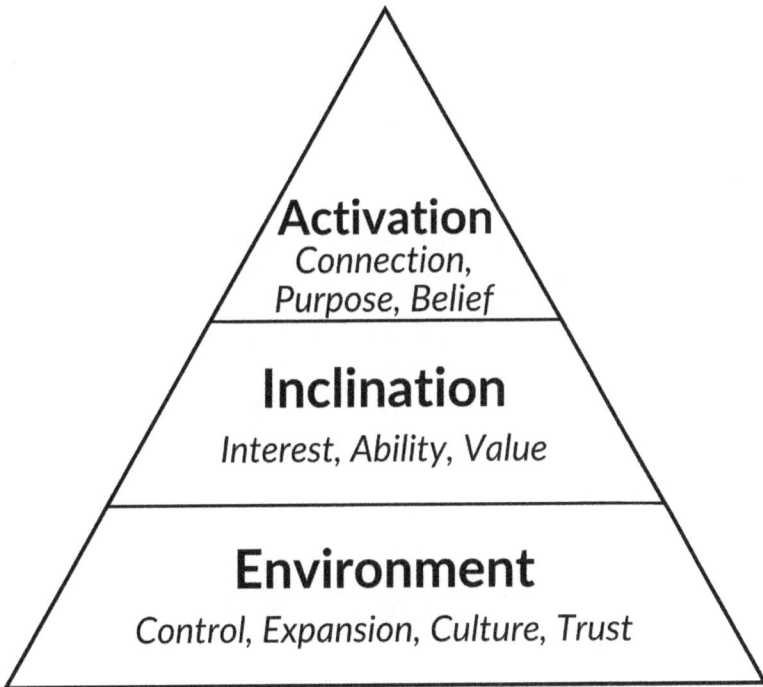

Activation
Connection,
Purpose, Belief

Inclination
Interest, Ability, Value

Environment
Control, Expansion, Culture, Trust

Chapter 17:
Team Engagement
Self-Reflection

When assessing your team's engagement, it may warrant a deep analysis of each of the elements in the Hierarchy of Team Engagement Needs. To help get you started, you may refer to this Team Engagement Self-Reflection as a quick start guide. It contains key questions related to each element in the hierarchy for a quick preliminary diagnosis. This self-reflection will assist in identifying what might be standing in the way of your team's engagement or where you might improve your efforts to boost engagement. When you're ready, you can conduct a self-reflection for your team by working through these guiding questions.

Environment: Can engagement thrive in this environment?	
Control	• Do team members feel that they have enough control over their work? • Do they have a sense of self-determination or are they experiencing reactance? • Do team members have a balance of support and autonomy?
Expansion	• Is there room for expansion? • Are there career growth and learning opportunities?
Culture	• Is there a culture of engagement (respect, failure safety, recognition, fairness, empathy / understanding)?
Trust	• Is there trust and reliability?

Inclination: Is my team inclined for the work?	
Interest	• Is the team interested in their work?
Ability	• Do they have the ability? • Have I helped them build the skills they need? • Do they have the capacity to perform (skill + capacity) and successfully achieve objectives?
Value	• Are their values aligned? (Have you considered generational values and personal values?)

Activation: Has the team been activated?	
Connection	<ul><li>Do team members feel a sense of connection?</li><li>Is there transparency?</li><li>Is there a consistent effort to maintain connection through regular team building, for example?</li></ul>
Purpose	<ul><li>Is the purpose and direction clear?</li><li>Is the purpose meaningful?</li><li>Is there a connection between shared purpose and personal purpose?</li></ul>
Belief	<ul><li>Is there self-efficacy? (Do the team members believe in themselves?)</li><li>Do the leaders believe in the team?</li><li>Are there strong enough shared beliefs?</li></ul>

Even with the most highly engaged teams, one thing might still stand in the way: attitude.

Chapter 18:
The Attitude Trap

I've worked on many project teams, each being a vastly different experience, not because of the project but because of the team. Many years ago, on one project in particular, our goal was to organize a celebratory gala for approximately 200 guests. What stands out about this experience was the engagement of every single team member. Everyone was deeply invested in hosting the best damn gala possible. The environment was right. There was a sense of control, a sense of trust, opportunities for future expansion, and a great working culture. Inclination was there. The entire team was highly interested, very able, and truly valued the work that we were doing. And finally, there was activation. The group had a strong purpose, the members were connected with one another, and they believed that the outcome would truly be great. However, one team member—though actively engaged—brought with them a bad attitude. Albeit, they brought unique insights and knowledge to the team and were always willing to go above and beyond. Even so, they brought a sense of resentfulness from their past experiences and were generally disgruntled. It was coarse comments in meetings, thorny emails, and fingers being pointed. At first, due to the high engagement of the rest of the team, we were able to manage just fine. Though as time went on, this one team member, little by little, was able to chip away at the rest of the team's morale, anchoring the team engagement down. Although the gala was successful, by the end, every team member was exhausted, frustrated, and ready to quit the team on account of the difficulty of dealing with this one person.

In a situation where you have attended to every level in the Hierarchy of Team Engagement Needs, there is still one trap you will need to look out for: attitude.

It is far easier to change someone's skill level than it is to change their attitude.

The saying "Hire for Attitude, Train for Skill" has merit. We have measures for improving one's skill level through training, coaching, and experience. Attitude, however, is much harder to change. One's attitude is a decided way of thinking, feeling, and approach. It is a result of their perspectives about their past experiences and encounters. When that attitude is negative, it inevitably shows up in their behaviour, their communication, and their overall presence. This negative energy doesn't exist in isolation—it wears on the mood and the productivity of everyone around them. That's why attitude is something we must not overlook. It is a potential hazard to your efforts in cultivating team engagement.

Let's say that you've created a high-performing environment, aligned inclination, and have made an effort to activate your team. Despite these efforts, there is one team member who refuses to get on board. Evidently, they have a negative attitude. How do you change their perspective to see the glass half-full when they so adamantly believe it's half-empty?

Before writing them off, it's worthwhile to investigate if this bad attitude is simply misplaced frustration from something else. Could it be...

Personal Issues

- Are they experiencing relationship or marital problems?
- Do they have family stress, like caring for sick family members? Parenting difficulties?
- Do they have any physical or mental health issues?
- Are they suffering from substance abuse or addiction?

Work-Related Stress

- Are they feeling overwhelmed by an increased workload?
- Are they feeling undervalued or unappreciated for their efforts?
- Are they going through conflict with colleagues or management? Is there unresolved tension?

Burnout

- Have they been experiencing prolonged periods of stress?
- Are they struggling to balance work demands with their personal life?

Life Changes

- Are they experiencing economic hardships or unexpected financial burdens?
- Are they experiencing any grief or loss? The death of a loved one, a breakup, or another major life event?
- Are they experiencing the emotional or logistical stress of moving or relocating?

Understanding what might be causing changes in their attitude creates opportunities to offer support and empathy. Are there any accommodations that can be made? Are there resources that could help? Even small efforts to understand the root of the issue can open the door to meaningful dialogue. Sometimes, just demonstrating that you care enough to offer support could be enough to create positive attitude changes.

On the other hand, there are instances in which none of these adverse life circumstances apply, and someone is simply resolute on being:

- Jaded
- Cynical
- Resentful
- Disgruntled
- Pessimistic
- Defiant
- Moody
- Complacent
- Hostile
- Uncooperative
- Entitled

In this case, the bottom line is that you've tried multiple strategies: cultivating a positive team environment, carefully aligning the team's abilities, promoting shared beliefs, checking in to support team members, and more. But with a bad attitude, these team members undermine any effort for improvement. Bad attitude produces poor engagement economics.

Pro Tip: Consider the Costs of Bad Attitude

Understanding the relationship between individual performance and a person's impact on team performance is important to help you make tough decisions about who should stay on the team. In the following chart, performance is plotted over time. The individual performance of a team member with a bad attitude often remains constant (or decreases over time). Bad attitude stands in the way of their own potential growth. However, this bad attitude doesn't just stagnate their own performance; it impacts the team's performance. Bad attitude creates difficulties for collaboration, slows progress on projects, undermines innovation, and burdens the rest of the team. If bad attitude is left unchecked for long enough, the negative impact of their presence on the team outweighs any individual value that they have. Over time, this team member will reduce the effectiveness and performance of the team as a whole.

Impact of Bad Attitude on Team Performance

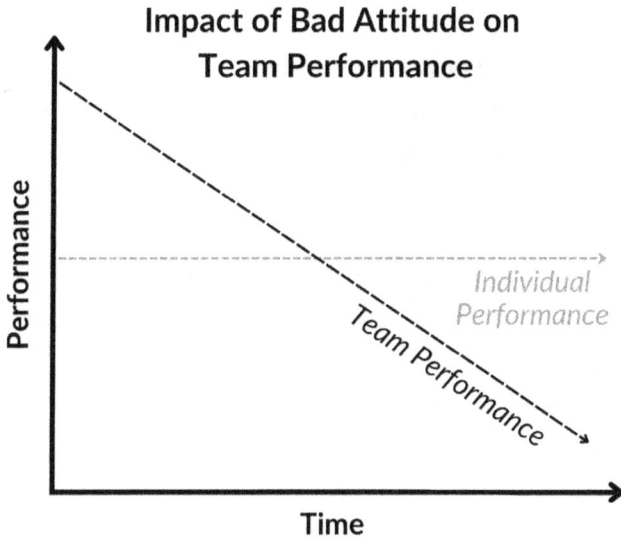

Seeing this impact over time makes it very clear that tolerating bad attitude is bad for the team. The tough part, the real *trap*, is when that team member with a bad attitude has tenure or is a high performer. It is common for high-performing individuals to get away with a bad attitude because leaders don't want to lose the results that person brings. And parting ways with a tenured individual can carry substantial financial implications for an organization. For those reasons, leaders find themselves *trapped* into putting up with bad attitude. The problem is that it is easy to measure the cost of losing this individual. It is not so easy to measure the cost of keeping them.

- How do you measure how disengaged other employees become due to the attitude of one individual?
- How do you measure the strain on mental health?
- How do you measure the time your team spends avoiding that one person?
- How do you measure the time a team needs to decompress following an interaction with this team member?
- How do you measure the extra time it takes for the team to reach a decision because one person's attitude slows down the process?
- How do you measure the difference between what a team could achieve and what it actually achieves when one person's negative attitude is holding them back?

Although difficult to measure, seeing the symptoms of a team member's bad attitude should be a red flag. It signals that if nothing changes, team engagement and, ultimately, team performance will be impacted over time. Every investment reaches a point of diminishing returns, where the costs outweigh the benefits and the return on investment no longer justifies any further effort. Ultimately, if a team member is unwilling to change and continues to cling to a bad attitude without reason, your time, energy, and resources will yield little to no return on investment. Bad attitude always erodes engagement and team performance. Your time, energy, and resources would be better spent on initiatives for people who are coachable and willing to grow.

Investing in all elements of the *Hierarchy of Team Engagement Needs,* paired with the *right attitude,* will yield positive **engagement economics**, generating spectacular results in performance and profitability.

Conclusion

Leadership is a tough gig. As leaders, we're often unprepared to lead a team while faced with enormous pressure to deliver results. We can take comfort in the fact that these challenges are universal. Leaders from all over the world are struggling with the very same things. With such pressures, even well-intentioned leaders often focus on quantitative metrics, like revenue, number of deals closed, or output rates. While these metrics matter, they are lagging indicators.[114] They are the result of the input and effort of **your team**. Therefore, your team is the leading indicator. Their collective effort and expertise create value and profitability. How much value? That is determined by their engagement and the associated discretionary effort.

Disengagement, or the lack of discretionary effort, is costing our organizations and our global economy. Disengagement's direct impact on performance is a drain on money, time, and resources. It restricts revenue, the number of deals closed, and the very output metrics that are constantly measured. Engagement, therefore, is not just a lofty idea; it is an economic and business strategy.

However, typical engagement initiatives often fall short. That's because they often miss the mark on what our teams actually need for their engagement. Another pizza lunch won't solve the fact that a team feels stuck and stagnant in their roles. Employee of the Month certificates won't eliminate feelings of resentment from unfair treatment. When engagement initiatives fail to consider a team's fundamental engagement needs, they come across as disjointed and are ineffective. So, instead of treating them as "nice-to-have" activities, they should be targeted strategies aimed at meeting your team's engagement needs.

The Hierarchy of Team Engagement Needs helps us identify what we're missing. Instead of being left scratching our heads and wondering what's going wrong, we can use it to assess whether the team's needs are being met. It is a tool to help you direct your strategy to the very needs that generate a return on investment in the form of performance and profitability.

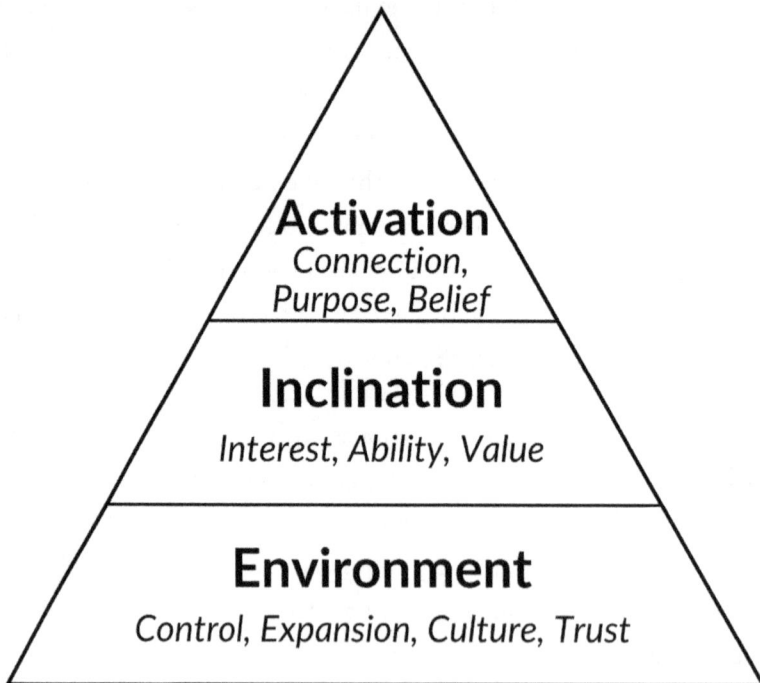

Activation
*Connection,
Purpose, Belief*

Inclination
Interest, Ability, Value

Environment
Control, Expansion, Culture, Trust

To maximize engagement economics, teams need an **environment** that promotes engagement. That is, one that gives them a sense of *control* in the form of supported autonomy, the ability to *expand* and grow, a positive *culture* characterized by respect, failure safety, recognition, fairness, empathy, and understanding, and also high levels of *trust*. Teams need to be **inclined** for their work. This means being *interested* in their work, having the *ability* to tackle challenges, and being aligned in their *values*. Finally, teams need to be **activated**. They need to feel a sense of *connection* and belonging, a sense of *purpose,* and they must also *believe* in successful outcomes.

These needs are universal. We *all* want to work in a great environment, we naturally wish to be inclined for our work, and we all long to be activated. Unless a bad attitude stands in the way, we all want to be **engaged** and fulfill our potential by performing at our best. For that to happen, our engagement needs must be met.

The point is that if performance and profitability are important to your organization, engagement should be too. Employee engagement is an important leading indicator for profitability and performance. So, while making strategic plans for the success of your business, don't forget about your most important asset: your people.

Equipped with the knowledge of what truly drives engagement, you now have the power to build better, more engaged, and more high-performing teams and experience all that positive **engagement economics** has to offer. The question is, what are you going to do with it?

I wish you good luck.
-Diondra

Continue the Conversation

If you'd like to continue the conversation, connect with the author, learn more, or book keynote speaking / training, you may use the channels below:

CONNECT ONLINE

- LinkedIn: linkedin.com/in/diondrafilicetti/
- Websites: engagementeconomics.com and drivenbyco.com
- Social Media: @drivenbyco & @engagementeconomics

WATCH DIONDRA'S TEDX TALKS

Unlocking team success: 5 crucial environmental factors | Diondra Filicetti | TEDxOshawa

https://www.youtube.com/watch?v=7mxsA9cNPFo&t=212s

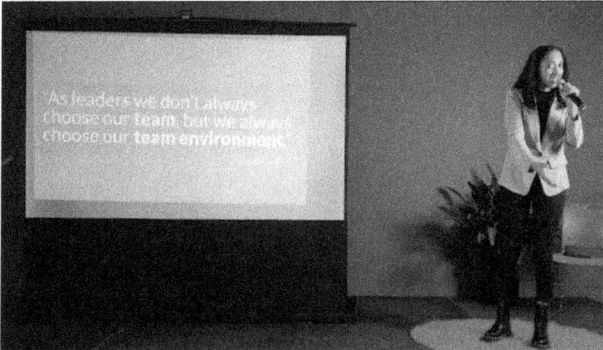

How to develop engaged and motivated teams | Diondra Filicetti | TEDxEtobicoke

https://www.youtube.com/watch?v=00x4GcQL5B0

Acknowledgements

To those who shared their stories, supported the writing process, and helped make this book possible.

- J. Bell
- M. Boake
- A. Chappelle
- T. Chrissis
- D. Clarke
- L. Desouza
- H. Ebadi
- K. Filicetti
- C. Gantioqui
- A. Gibson
- M. Gnatek
- B. Horvath
- R. Huitema
- J. Jaskowski
- C. Maclean
- N. Mainville
- D. Murray
- J. Peryer-Reid
- M. Raad
- P. Reid
- D. Shaffer
- R. Touma
- K. Steward
- J. Wallace
- J. Wardle
- M. Wilks

And others who wished to remain anonymous.

About the Author

Photo Credit: Sheldon Isaac Photography

Diondra Filicetti is a distinguished learning and development professional, an experienced training facilitator, instructor, and two-time TEDx speaker specializing in team engagement strategy, leadership effectiveness, and self-awareness. With a background in adult learning and instructional design, and a Bachelor of Technology, Diondra uniquely blends educational theory with practical application to create transformative learning experiences.

Notes

Introduction

[1] *State of the Global Workplace: The Voice of the World's Employees – Research Summary,* Gallup, https://www.gallup.com/workplace/349484/state-of-the-global-workplace.aspx.

[2] Adam Hayes, *Economics Defined with Types, Indicators and Systems,* Investopedia, last updated June 28. 2024, https://www.investopedia.com/terms/e/economics.asp.

Chapter 1

[3] Elysse Bell, *Henry Ford: American Industrialist and Founder of Ford Motor Company,* Investopedia, last updated March 27, 2025, https://www.investopedia.com/henry-ford-5225035#:~:text=He%20invented%20several%20vehicles%2C%20most,assembly%20line%20to%20car%20production.

[4] *Moving Assembly Line,* Ford Motor Company, retrieved November 8, 2024 from https://corporate.ford.com/articles/history/moving-assembly-line.html.

[5] Elysse Bell, *Henry Ford: American Industrialist and Founder of Ford Motor Company,* Investopedia, last updated March 27, 2025, https://www.investopedia.com/henry-ford-5225035#:~:text=He%20invented%20several%20vehicles%2C%20most,assembly%20line%20to%20car%20production.

[6] Masumi R. Izawa, Michael D. French, Alan Hedge, "Shining New Light on the Hawthorne Illumination Experiments," *Human Factors,* October 2011, vol. 53, no. 5, pp. 528-547, doi: 10.1177/0018720811417968.

[7] Ayesh Perera, *Hawthorne Effect in Psychology: Experimental Studies,* Simply Psychology, last updated February 13, 2024, https://www.simplypsychology.org/hawthorne-effect.html.

[8] Jo Olsen, *Creating a High-Performance Workplace by Tapping into Discretionary Effort,* HR Magazine, last updated February 25, 2021, https://www.hrmagazine.co.uk/content/comment/creating-a-high-performance-workplace-by-tapping-into-discretionary-effort/.

[9] *Employee Engagement Drives Growth,* Gallup, last updated January 7, 2023, https://www.gallup.com/workplace/236927/employee-engagement-drives-growth.aspx.

[10] Lee Waters, *How to Encourage Discretionary Effort Beyond the Bare Minimum,* C2Perform, https://www.c2perform.com/blog/what-is-discretionary-effort-how-to-encourage-it.

[11] *Control, Opportunity, & Leadership: A Study of Employee Engagement in the Canadian Workplace*, Psychometrics Canada Ltd., retrieved from https://spinify.com/wp-content/uploads/2019/10/engagement_study.pdf.

[12] Brian J. Brim, Dana Williams, Jennifer Robison, *Defeat Employee Loneliness and Worry with CliftonStrengths*, Gallup, last updated April 21, 2020, https://www.gallup.com/cliftonstrengths/en/308939/defeat-employee-loneliness-worry-cliftonstrengths.aspx.

[13] Victor Lipman, *Surprising, Disturbing Facts from the Mother of all Employee Engagement Surveys*, Forbes, last updated July 30, 2015, https://www.forbes.com/sites/victorlipman/2013/09/23/surprising-disturbing-facts-from-the-mother-of-all-employee-engagement-surveys/.

[14] Jim Harter, *Employee Engagement vs. Employee Satisfaction and Organizational Culture*, Gallup, last updated August 13, 2022, https://www.gallup.com/workplace/236366/right-culture-not-employee-satisfaction.aspx.

[15] Jim Harter, *3 Key Insights into the Global Workplace*, Gallup, last updated June 12, 2024, https://www.gallup.com/workplace/645416/key-insights-global-workplace.aspx.

[16] *State of the Global Workplace: The Voice of the World's Employees – Research Summary*, Gallup, retrieved from https://www.gallup.com/workplace/349484/state-of-the-global-workplace.aspx.

[17] *State of the Global Workplace: The Voice of the World's Employees – Research Summary*, Gallup.

Chapter 2

[18] Tom Nolan, Jane Smith, *The No. 1 Employee Benefit that No One's Talking About*, Gallup, retrieved from https://www.gallup.com/workplace/232955/no-employee-benefit-no-one-talking.aspx.

[19] Bryan Robinson, Ph. D. *Why Managers May Have a Bigger Mental-Health Impact than your Therapist*, Forbes, last updated April 15, 2024, https://www.forbes.com/sites/bryanrobinson/2024/04/15/number-1-reason-managers-have-a-bigger-mental-health-impact-than-your-therapist/.

[20] *State of the American Manager*, Gallup, retrieved from https://www.gallup.com/services/182138/state-american-manager.aspx.

[21] *Bad Boss Index: 1,000 Employees Name Worst Manager Behaviors*, BambooHR, last updated March 18, 2019, https://www.bamboohr.com/blog/bad-boss-index-the-worst-boss-behaviors-according-to-employees-infographic.

[22] *More than One-Quarter of Managers Said They Weren't Ready to Lead When They Began Managing Others, Finds New Careerbuilder Survey*, Career Builder, last updated March 28, 2011, https://www.prnewswire.com/news-releases/more-than-one-quarter-of-managers-said-they-werent-ready-to-lead-when-they-began-managing-others-finds-new-careerbuilder-survey-118761504.html.

[23] Tom Nolan, Jane Smith, *The No. 1 Employee Benefit that No One's Talking Abou.t*

[24] William Gentry, Regina Eckert, Sarah Stawiski, Sophia Zhao, *The Challenges Leaders Face Around the World: More Similar than Different*, Center for Creative Leadership, retrieved from https://cclinnovation.org/wp-content/uploads/2020/03/challengesleadersface.pdf

Chapter 3

[25] Saul McLeod, *Maslow's Hierarchy of Needs*. Simply Psychology, retrieved January 28, 2023, from https://www.simplypsychology.org/maslow.html

Chapter 4

[26] Greg Iacurci, *2022 Was the "Real Year of the Great Resignation, Says Economist,"* CNBC, last updated February 1, 2023, https://www.cnbc.com/2023/02/01/why-2022-was-the-real-year-of-the-great-resignation.html#:~:text=About%2050.5%20million%20people%20quit,to%20leave%20the%20workforce%20altogether.

[27] Donald Sull, Charles Sull, Ben Zweig, *Toxic Culture Is Driving the Great Resignation*, MIT Sloan Management Review, last updated January 11, 2022, https://sloanreview.mit.edu/article/toxic-culture-is-driving-the-great-resignation/.

[28] Frederico Lourenco, BJ Casey, "Adjusting Behavior to Changing Environmental Demands with Development," *Neurosci Biobehav* Rev. 2013 Nov;37(9 Pt B):2233-42, retrieved from https://pmc.ncbi.nlm.nih.gov/articles/PMC3751996/.

Chapter 5

[29] Justin A. Wellman, Andrew L. Geers, "Rebel Without a (conscious) Cause: Priming a Nonconscious Goal for Psychological Reactance. *Basic and Applied Social Psychology*, 31(1), 9-16, https://doi.org/10.1080/01973530802659711

[30] Ricky Wilcocks, The Damaging Impact of Micromanagement and How to End It, Redline Group, last updated January 9, 2023, https://www.redlinegroup.com/insight-details/the-damaging-impact-of-micromanagement-and-how-to-end-it#:~:text=Micromanagement%20can%20lead%20to%20decreased,to%20handle%20their%20responsibilities%20independently.

[31] Marylène Gagné, Edward Deci, "Self-Determination Theory and Work Motivation," *Journal of Organizational Behavior, 26*(3), 331–362, https://doi.org/10.1002/job.322. Retrieved from https://selfdetermination-theory.org/SDT/documents/2005_GagneDeci_JOB_SDTtheory.pdf.

[32] Michael Mankins, Eric Garton, *How Spotify Balances Employee Autonomy and Accountability*, Harvard Business Review, last updated February 9, 2017, https://hbr.org/2017/02/how-spotify-balances-employee-autonomy-and-accountability.

Chapter 6

[33] Wikipedia, The Free Encyclopedia, *JaMarcus Russell*, last modified March 16, 2025. Accessed October 20, 2025. https://en.wikipedia.org/wiki/JaMarcus_Russell.

[34] Adam Lazarus, *The 50 Best College Players Who Flopped in the NFL*, Bleacher Report, February 4, 2011, https://bleacherreport.com/articles/596944-the-50-best-college-players-who-flopped-in-the-nfl.

[35] Wikipedia, The Free Encyclopedia Tom Brady. last modified June 28, 2025. Accessed June 29, 2024. https://en.wikipedia.org/wiki/Tom_Brady.

[36] Eric Adelson, *Tom Brady's Guru*, ThePostGame.com, January 11, 2011, archived September 9, 2018, https://web.archive.org/web/20180909185451/http://www.thepostgame.com/features/201101/tom-bradys-guru.

[37] Barry Ryan, *Employee Retention Statistics 2025: The Ultimate Guide*, Thirst, last updated January 14, 2025, https://thirst.io/blog/employee-retention-statistics-2025.

[38] Ed Catmull, *How Pixar Fosters Collective Creativity*, Harvard Business Review, last updated September 2008, https://hbr.org/2008/09/how-pixar-fosters-collective-creativity

Chapter 7

[39] Kerm Henriksen, Elizabeth Dayton, "Organizational Silence and Hidden Threats to Patient Safety," *Health Services Research*, 41(4 Pt 2), 1539–1554, retrieved from https://doi.org/10.1111/j.1475-6773.2006.00564.x.

[40] *Equity Theory*, Gartner, retrieved May 20, 2025, from https://www.gartner.com/en/human-resources/glossary/equity-theory.

[41] Kristen Robertson, *3 Inspiring Organizational Culture Change Examples*, The Predictive Index, last updated July 8, 2020, https://www.predictiveindex.com/blog/organizational-culture-change-examples/

[42] *Mental Health—Psychosocial Risk Factors in the Workplace*, Canadian Centre for Occupational Health and Safety, retrieved from https://www.ccohs.ca/oshanswers/psychosocial/mh/mentalhealth_risk.html

[43] *Why It's Advantageous to Allow Failure into your Workplace*, Tandem HR, retrieved from https://tandemhr.com/why-its-advantageous-to-allow-failure-into-your-workplace/.

[44] Coby Skonord, *Post-it Notes: An Innovative Employee Idea that Was Originally a Mistake*, Ideawake, last updated February 9, 2021, https://ideawake.com/post-it-notes-employee-idea-that-was-originally-mistake/#:~:text=The%20Post%2Dit%20Note%20Was,easily%20be%20removed%20without%20residue

[45] *History Timeline: Post-it Notes*, Post-It, retrieved from https://www.post-it.com/3M/en_US/post-it/contact-us/about-us/

[46] *History Timeline: Post-it Notes,* Post-It.

[47] *Why It's Advantageous to Allow Failure into your Workplace*, Tandem HR, retrieved from https://tandemhr.com/why-its-advantageous-to-allow-failure-into-your-workplace/.

[48] *The Importance of Employee Recognition: Low Cost, High Impact*, Gallup, last updated June 18, 2016,https://www.gallup.com/workplace/236441/employee-recognition-low-cost-high-impact.aspx.

[49] *Employee Recognition: 5 Ways to Recognize your Employees*, Haiilo, last updated January 5, 2023, https://haiilo.com/blog/5-ways-to-recognize-employees/

[50] *Insurance Company: Elevating Culture with Recognition*, O.C. Tanner, retrieved April 8, 2025 from https://www.octanner.com/en-gb/client-stories/insurance-company.

[51] *Insurance company: Elevating culture with recognition*, O C. Tanner .

[52] Lauren Desouza, CEO and founder, Ace, in discussion with the author, March 2024.

[53] Lauren Desouza, CEO and founder, Ace.

Chapter 8

[54] Bozi Tatarevic, B, *4 Tires & Fuel: Pit Crews Handle the Pressure at Las Vegas*, Racing America, last updated March 4, 2024, https://racingamerica.com/news/nascar/4-tires-fuel-vegas#.

[55] Becky Greiner, *The Unsung Heroes of NASCAR: A Closer Look at the Pit Crew Roles & Rules,* The Daily Downforce, retrieved from https://dailydownforce.com/nascar-pit-crew-roles-and-rules/#:~:text=those%20are%20the%20fire%20pit,the%20head%20Coach%20in%20NASCAR.

[56] Simon Sinek, *What's More Important: TRUST or PERFORMANCE?*, posted June 1, 2022, YouTube, 3 min., 2 sec., https://www.youtube.com/watch?v=UoHA68Xxp4w

[57] Simon Sinek, *What's More Important.*

[58] *Trusted Communication Changes Everything*, FranklinCovey, retrieved from https://www.franklin-covey.com/blog/trusted-communication-changes-everything/.

[59] *Netflix Culture—The Best Work of Our Lives*, Netflix jobs, retrieved June 27, 2024 from https://jobs.net-flix.com/culture.

Chapter 9

[60] Sarah Berger, *Oprah Winfrey: This Is the Moment My "Job Ended" and My "Calling Began,"* CNBC, last updated April 1, 2019, https://www.cnbc.com/2019/04/01/how-oprah-winfrey-found-her-calling.html.

Chapter 10

[61] Gary Vee, *Your "Laziness" Is Telling You Something*, posted August 12, 2022, YouTube, 42 sec., https://www.youtube.com/watch?v=M6REvbBQtto.

[62] Annie Murphy Paul, *How the Power of Interest Drives Learning*, KQED, last updated November 4, 2013, https://www.kqed.org/mindshift/32503/how-the-power-of-interest-drives-learning.

[63] Annie Murphy Paul, *How the Power of Interest Drives Learning.*

[64] *50+ CRM statistics & trends you should know in 2024*, FreshWorks, last updated August 5, 2024, https://www.freshworks.com/theworks/insights/crm-statistics/.

Chapter 11

[65] Lyle Daly, L. (2024, August). *The largest companies by market cap in 2024.* The Motley Fool, last updated June 4, 2025, https://www.fool.com/research/largest-companies-by-market-cap/#:~:text=Ap-ple%20is%20the%20largest%20company,and%20Amazon%20(%241.95%20trillion).

[66] Zac Francis, *3 Takeaways from Apple's Retail Store Employee Training*, eduMe, retrieved from https://www.edume.com/blog/how-apple-trains-its-retail-employees#Apple-retail-training

[67] Zac Francis, *3 Takeaways from Apple's Retail Store Employee Training.*

[68] Zac Francis, *3 Takeaways from Apple's Retail Store Employee Training.*

[69] Kailash Ganesh, *What Is Retail Employee Turnover Rate: Top Causes and Strategies to Tackle It*, CultureMonkey, last updated May 14, 2024, https://www.culturemonkey.io/employee-engagement/retail-employee-turnover-rate/#:~:text=On%20average%2C%20retail%20turnover%20hovers,within%20a%20year%2C%20reports%20McKinsey.

[70] *What We Do: Deloitte*, Deloitte, retrieved from https://www.deloitte.com/global/en/what-we-do.html?icid=top_what-we-do.

[71] *Deloitte Ranked No. 1 Consulting Service Provider Worldwide by Revenue in Gartner® Market Share Report*, last updated July 12, 2023, https://www.deloitte.com/global/en/about/recognition/analyst-relations/deloitte-ranked-no-1-consulting-service-provider-worldwide-by-revenue-according-to-gartner.html.

[72] *Deloitte University (DU) North*, Deloitte Canada, retrieved from https://www2.deloitte.com/ca/en/pages/careers/topics/du-north-vision-grow-extraordinary-leaders.html.

[73] *Nick Nurse Shares His Unique Coaching Philosophy That's Somehow Both Player and Team Friendly*, created by The Young Man and the Three, posted January 4, 2022, 4 min., 33 sec., YouTube. https://www.youtube.com/watch?v=-F7DK7jfwO8.

[74] *Nick Nurse Shares His Unique Coaching Philosophy*.

Chapter 12

[75] Jason Richmond, J, *Cultivating Loyalty: Employee Retention Strategies for the Younger Generations*. Forbes, retrieved August 13, 2024, from https://www.forbes.com/councils/forbesbusinesscouncil/2024/02/20/cultivating-loyalty-employee-retention-strategies-for-the-younger-generations/.

[76] Jennifer Morehead, *Navigating the Changing Landscape of Employee Retention*, last updated December 4, 2024, https://trainingmag.com/navigating-the-changing-landscape-of-employee-retention/.

[77] Hanju Lee, *The Changing Generational Values*, Johns Hopkins University, last updated November 17, 2022, https://imagine.jhu.edu/blog/2022/11/17/the-changing-generational-values/.

[78] *Gen Z vs. Gen Alpha: What's the Difference?* Greenlight, retrieved April 21, 2025, from https://greenlight.com/learning-center/fun-facts/gen-z-vs-gen-alpha.
[79] *Gen Z vs. Gen Alpha: What's the Difference?*

[80] Kendra Cherry, *Cognitive Dissonance and the Discomfort of Holding Conflicting Beliefs*, Verywell Mind, last updated January 27, 2025, https://www.verywellmind.com/what-is-cognitive-dissonance-2795012.

[81] Kendra Cherry, *Left Brain vs. Right Brain Dominance*. Verywell Mind., last updated March 7, 2024, https://www.verywellmind.com/left-brain-vs-right-brain-2795005.

[82] *Affective Commitment: Definition and Explanation*, The Oxford Review, retrieved April 23, 2025, from https://oxford-review.com/the-oxford-review-dei-diversity-equity-and-inclusion-dictionary/affective-commit-ment-definition-and-explanation/.

[83] *Affective Commitment: Definition and Explanation*.

Chapter 13

[84] *Make Your Bed—Adm. William McRaven, University of Texas, 2014*, UniversityKart, posted on May 19, 2024, 19 min., 26 sec., YouTube,https://www.youtube.com/watch?v=lu0HPSdgb-k.

Chapter 14

[85] *Denzel Washington University of Pennsylvania*, Vidbi, posted May 16, 2011, 22 min., 42 sec., YouTube. https://www.youtube.com/watch?v=JEFbfwg9dek.

[86] *Connection*, Encyclopedia.com, retrieved May 24, 2025, from https://www.encyclopedia.com/literature-and-arts/language-linguistics-and-literary-terms/english-vocabulary-d/connection.

[87] Suzan Bond, *When Orgs Become Siloed*, last updated February 9, 2024,Suzan's Fieldnotes, https://suzans-fieldnotes.substack.com/p/when-orgs-become-siloed.

[88] Olivia Bush, *Working from Home Statistics in Canada*, Made in CA, last updated January 4, 2025, https://madeinca.ca/working-from-home-canada-statistics/.

[89] Katherine Haan, Top *Remote Work Statistics and Trends*, Forbes, last updated June 12, 2023, https://www.forbes.com/advisor/business/remote-work-statistics/.

[90] DeAnne Aguirre, Micah Alpern, *10 Principles of Leading Change Management*, Strategy+Business, last up-dated June 6, 2014,https://www.strategy-business.com/article/00255.

[91] Brian Scudamore, *Why Team Building Is the Most Important Investment You'll Make*, Forbes, last updated March 9, 2016, https://www.forbes.com/sites/brianscudamore/2016/03/09/why-team-building-is-the-most-important-investment-youll-make/.

[92] Brian Scudamore, *Why Team Building Is the Most Important Investment You'll Make*.

Chapter 15

[93] *The Original Pioneers of Silicon Valley*, Hewlett-Packard Enterprise, retrieved October 4, 2024, from https://www.hpe.com/us/en/about/bill-dave.html.

[94] Bret Waters, *The "HP Way" and the Founding of Silicon Valley*, Medium, retrieved October 4, 2024, from https://bretwaters.medium.com/the-hp-way-and-the-founding-of-silicon-valley-33837a30af3d.

[95] *Driven by Purpose. Built on Results*, Creative Niche, retrieved from https://www.creativeniche.com/.

[96] Brian Bacon, *How Purpose Drives Performance in Organisations*, Oxford Leadership, retrieved from https://www.oxfordleadership.com/how-purpose-drives-performance-in-organisations/.

[97] *Terms, Commands & Glossary*, Kamloops Interior Dragons, retrieved October 6, 2024, from https://kamloopsinteriordragons.ca/terms-commands-glossary/.

[98] *Purpose, Vision and Values*, Royal Bank of Canada, retrieved from https://www.rbc.com/our-company/purpose-vision-and-values.html.

[99] Marcel Schwantes, *Science Says 92 Percent of People Don't Achieve their Goals. Here's How the Other 8 Percent Do,* Inc.com, last updated July 26, 2016, https://www.inc.com/marcel-schwantes/science-says-92-percent-of-people-dont-achieve-goals-heres-how-the-other-8-perce.html.

Chapter 16

[100] David Yates, *Harry Potter and the Half-Blood Prince,* film, Warner Bros. Pictures, 2009.

[101] Dale Schunk, "Self-efficacy, motivation, and performance," 1995, *Journal of Applied Sport Psychology*, 7(2), 112-137, retrieved from https://libres.uncg.edu/ir/uncg/f/D_Schunk_Self_1995.pdf.

[102] Anne-Laure Le Cunff, *The Pygmalion Effect: An Invisible Nudge Towards Success*, Ness Labs, last updated November 14, 2022, https://nesslabs.com/pygmalion-effect.

[103] Kyle Steward, Director of Business Development, in discussion with the author, April 2025.

[104] *The History of Tobacco Marketing,* Tobacco Stops With Me, retrieved from https://stopswithme.com/history-tobacco-marketing-scary-story/#:~:text=In%20the%201950s%20and%202060s,fantasies%20of%20manliness%20and%20independence.

[105] Shobit Seth, *The BlackBerry Story: Constant Success and Failure*, Investopedia, last updated March 7, 2025, https://www.investopedia.com/articles/investing/062315/blackberry-story-constant-success-failure.asp.

[106] Shobit Seth, *The BlackBerry Story: Constant Success and Failure.*

[107] *The Fall of BlackBerry: How Ignoring Innovation Led to Decline*, Time for Designs, last updated October 10, 2023, https://www.timefordesigns.com/blog/2023/10/10/the-fall-of-blackberry-how-ignoring-innovation-led-to-decline/.

[108] James Kaatz, *Marketing Rule of 7's*, Marketing Illumination, last updated Feb 3, 2025, https://www.marketingillumination.com/blogs/marketing-rule-of-7s.

[109] Adam Judelson, *The Unconventional Palantir Principles that Catalyzed a Generation of Startups*, Lenny's Newsletter, last updated June 13, 2023,https://www.lennysnewsletter.com/p/the-unconventional-palantir-principles.

Activation Key Takeaways: Where There's Activation, There's a Way

[110] *What was the Space Race?* National Air and Space Museum | Smithsonian, last updated August 23, 2023, https://airandspace.si.edu/stories/editorial/what-was-space-race.

[111] Amy Stamm, *We Choose to Go to the Moon" and other Apollo Speeches,* National Air and Space Museum | Smithsonian, last updated July 17, 2019, https://airandspace.si.edu/stories/editorial/we-choose-go-moon-and-other-apollo-speeches.

[112] Marcia Dunn, *Apollo 11 Moon Landing Had Thousands Working Behind Scenes,* CityNews Halifax, last updated July 15, 2019, https://halifax.citynews.ca/2019/07/15/apollo-11-moon-landing-had-thousands-working-behind-scenes/.
[113] Sarah Loff, *Apollo 11 Mission Overview.* NASA, last updated April 17, 2015, https://www.nasa.gov/history/apollo-11-mission-overview/.

Conclusion

[114] Lisa Earle McLeod, *Need your Team to Perform? Start with Belief*, Forbes, last updated May 1, 2020, https://www.forbes.com/sites/lisaearlemcleod/2020/04/30/need-your-team-to-perform-start-with-belief/.